OPERATION: WIRED DIFFERENTLY

JON A. ARCHAMBAULT

ISBN: 978-1-7776471-0-0

To those who still fight in the streets or overseas,
stay safe brothers and sisters.

To those who are bunkered at home,
unlock the front door,
you are not alone.

To all those who have served and still serve,
thank you for your service.

Link to my playlist, The War Within, created for this book:

https://open.spotify.com/playlist/7Jmt6iMidC7pkjB077B2nT?si=TieuG036QkuMgG5dVXeK0w

CONTENTS

In the nice restaurant…
Perfect for romancing my love,
I have to sit with my back to the wall.

I register two exits.
Staff and clients combined number 26.
I analyze their behavior,
While partially attending my wife,
Who I am keenly aware,
Feels my absence.

She suffers in silence.
She married a man in uniform,
Knows its threads are woven into me,
Beneath my trendy jeans and soft, civilian pullover.

After our dinner date,
We will drive home,
And,
At all times,
I will know the make and model behind us,
How many passengers,
The distance they follow,
See them as clearly as my steady hand which rests on the wheel.

Last year, when she gave birth to our son,
When I followed her magnificent body down the hospital hallway,
My vision faded for a moment or five,
And I saw a man who'd been shot,
In a gang war, Over territory.

Tomorrow, she will see the beauty in the park near our house,
Nature in full glory,
And marvel over the size of a maple.
I might even carve our initials in its trunk,
But before I can get to the heart that surrounds us,
I will remember the man who was stabbed,
Because he refused to give up his wallet.

Peace is preceded by negotiation and active duty,
Even when it appears that it has simply been established.
While the contract (of peace) has been signed, sealed, and delivered,
To ensure a safe land, with protected borders,
The bargain is maintained,
By the career soldier,
In situations,
Unknown to,
Joe Canada.

Without the uniform,
The one worn for every-single-citizen-in-Canada,
(For this land is your land and this land is my land, this land was made for you and me),
I still carry the weight.

I signed up to serve my country,
For the greater good…
To die for her.

And today…
I cannot rediscover my home,
Because it appears that,
Injustice is omnipresent.

In that place,
Where I had a certain haircut,
Was obliged to timing,
Lived according to rules,
There was order.
Each person walked the line.
Or didn't.

In this place,
Where I can wear my hair as I like,
Can show up late,
Slip in and out of protocol (what protocol?),
There is chaos.
People continuously line-crossing,
Speeding wantonly,
Violating indiscriminately,
Stealing shamelessly, without penalty.

People want to fix me.
Correct me from pointing out violations of civility.

And something is wrong with me?

I put a smile on my lips,
To seem like everyone else,
Because I know what I need to show,
So nobody worries for me.

And,
With a pride in my heart, that is like the sun except bigger and brighter.

With a respect so deep that the roots of the maple in the park,
could never reach such depths.

With a sense of honour that could make the hardest of hard weep with joy.

With a sense of awe for those heroes who continue to serve in life-time careers.

For our military, there I go:
Walking around with a rear-view mirror in my hand,
Marching with my military brothers who keep step in their parts of,
This-land-is-our-land.

To the psychologist's office,
Where I will be asked to lay down my shield,
Encouraged to release the demons,
That served to protect me so that I could protect you,
And create this thing we call peace.

OPERATION WIRED DIFFERENTLY

BRIEFING ONE
OBJECTIVE: INTRODUCTION

J.A.-Archambault. Corporal H80 415 001

The pages ahead are an open disclosure, a voluntary release of my story, an open mic version of my life in a blend of three acts: factual narrative, prosaic essay, and poem, as I endeavour to inform.

I am compelled to share so that I can continue to serve my country, honour my colleagues and, perhaps, save lives… including my own.

Chronologically, I have much more future ahead of me than behind me. I'm young, yet I feel like I have already been through a full lifetime—decades—of soldierhood. I have referred to myself as being wired differently—a phrase I heard from a guy when I was in my twenties.

The Necessary Transformation

When civilians become soldiers, they are reprogrammed; individuals become a collective and identify as such—they know they are one. It is the only way the current military can be successful in its enterprises.

Soldiers depend on acting as a group for survival—without an 'all for one' programming, there would be no way to carry out the protection society requires. This is a process within militarization (not to be mistaken with a militaristic regime). When a country readies its troops, it must first train them. To be one.

Typically, civilians see the opposite of the team approach in movies: the rogue hero featured as a star operator ahead of the group. This is not the way it is. Soldiers act together in planned action.

All serving soldiers are used to a black and white world—right/wrong, yes/no, go/stop. Follow the rules. All the time.

Soldiers do not have a maybe. Maybe is grey.

The process of training a soldier removes the grey. There are no grey areas in the world of a soldier because grey allows for all kinds of lax interpretations of the rules—dangerous territory for trained elites.

When soldiers return from deployment, regardless of any degree of trauma experienced, they return to a grey world—a world of maybes. Civilian life **IS** grey. It's hard to come back and face maybe—when taking a pen from a bank is ***not*** stealing, when fifteen kilometres an hour over the speed limit is ***not*** speeding, even when ten-after-five is ***not*** five o'clock.

Black and White mindsets have a difficult time functioning in a grey community. Grey community members find Black and White operators almost impossible to live with. Grey is the majority. So, the solution: reprogram the Black and White. Majority rules.

Just how Black and White is the world of first responders? The military is absolute Black and White. The police exist in a mostly Black and White framework but are so intertwined with grey life that the structure has to be compatible with the grey of civilian society. Corrections officers—to remain safe—must exist in Black and White. There are aspects of emergency work that have to be Black and White, but co-exist in Grey. Note: when first responders are dealing with every-day public, the less Black and White they can be.

Calling Canadians To The Carpet

The term 'first responders' encompasses many groups. Each has its degree of Black and White. While I focus on my own area of expertise here in this book, the concepts are applicable to all those who serve and protect.

In my quest and request for people to understand Operational Stress Injury (OSI) and Post-traumatic Stress Disorder (PTSD), to grasp the role of first responders who are at risk for PTSD or have already been diagnosed with the effects of exposure to trauma, I want to give a boots on the ground account of what life is like. I'll share what I understand about first responders, how my own life has been drastically altered while I am only in my thirties, touch on the organizations with which I am involved, and assign a role to all Canadians so that they can begin the journey to assist those who put their lives on the line for safety and peace.

Checking In With You On A Human Response That Might Be Yours (and it's okay if it is... that's why I'm writing this book)

ONE: A soldier returns from a deployment with a missing limb; you meet him at a fundraiser for your child's basketball team; you stare a little; someone mentions an improvised explosive device (IED) and a country in the Middle East, throws in a 'saved his platoon' or 'prevented the massacre of women and children'. As a civilian, you run through a gamut of thoughts: that must have been painful, length of recovery, hero, selfless, nice guy… WOW. Wonder if he'd like to come to the bar-b-que we're having next weekend?

TWO: As a business owner in a rural area—a feed store—you have a customer who comes in for large bags of kibble for his dogs; the guy's always been a little quiet, but today he seems interested in a new product line. You get talking. He's ex-military or police; you're not sure because you sort of forgot what he said once he mentioned he found long hikes with his dogs to be therapeutic… helps his PTSD. The earth shifts under your feet. All your mind does is revolve around his stability—will you say something to set him off? What would trigger him? Trigger? You have a few guns locked in a showcase—for discouraging gophers and coyotes—should you move your body so he doesn't see them? Does he have other injuries you could focus on? Maybe something more like that guy you met at the school fundraiser, that hero… what with the improvised explosive incident and saving all those people.

You tap your foot. A part of you is like: don't know anything about this… don't know what to say. Another part of you is: okay, hurry up, get out of here, I don't want you going off on me.

You're in conflict. It was so much easier when you could see the injury in a way of not seeing the missing limb. What's missing in this guy? Does he take meds?

You're sweating. You're sure he knows you're thinking about him.

The parting is abrupt, not unfriendly, but there is an unspoken message: 'I'm afraid of you but I don't know why.' You feel like crap. But you won't be inviting him to the bar-b-que. Why? The guy loves dogs. You love dogs. Dogs are incredible companions. You know this because you turn to yours when you're stressed.

It's Okay, I'll Help You Understand

There is critical information that Joe Canada needs in order to understand first responders and those in the military. It begins with appreciating the roles that first responders are thrust into when they serve. It continues with building a comfort zone with a neighbour who is a first responder with PTSD or Operational Stress Injuries… so comfortable that you find yourself feeling the same as you do when you interact with the hero missing the limb.

If you are waiting for a way to answer your own call to duty, to serve your country, as a civilian, 'understanding' is one way you can make a massive difference. A willingness to understand has the potential to make you a gamechanger in the lives of others.

Investing to understand is a high calling, considering many official agencies do not know how to deal with 'those' individuals, and therefore cannot provide all the tools for recovery.

We can work together. As I see it, there are two main layers of 'need to grow, learn, and discover':

1) The general public doesn't have the information they need to comprehend what is happening even though there are increasing diagnoses of people affected by trauma.

2) Society has miles to go to ensure that future first responders are prepared for—even inoculated against, in some way, so as not to succumb to—the darkness of PTSD and related disorders.

Without progressive and innovative work, as long as there are positions that entail exposure to harrowing situations, PTSD will continue to be an issue. It could take many years to create a middle ground. A starter conversation is Canada's opportunity to lead the world in compassion and solution.

My duty to my country did not end with my military career; I continue to serve, writing for all the soldiers who cannot speak out and yet are deeply hurt. As long as it takes, I will work on an information flow to individuals, organizations, and the general public, regarding PTSD. I will continue to inform Canadians that the military and other first responders are wired differently, for it is in our differences that we can detect what is needed to collaborate, innovate, and create peace for each other and within ourselves.

There is a stigma attached to this word 'militaristic'. Negative examples in history whereby whole countries were regarded as being militaristic—think barbaric, inhumane. This is not the case with the Canadian military. It does not seek to influence the whole population into being militaristic toward the world. It carries out protective duties when and if Canada or other world bodies require assistance. The posture of the Canadian Forces is not an offensive one, even in pushback of militaristic countries.

Knowledge Is Key

I am a young man, a thorough researcher, and a born storyteller, writing a book that praises the military—and brings out the downside. I explain about civic policing, from the perspective of a police officer. One of the best ways to have this conversation is to take you inside my mind.

Come into my life. I welcome you here with all my heart.

Without the uniform, I still carry the weight…
Years ago, I signed up to serve my country,
For the greater good.
Willing to make the ultimate sacrifice.
I met a new family in those ranks.

We were all wearing this same uniform.
We were preaching for the same.
And our mission was the same.
We struggled together.
We were warriors.

Today, we are spread across the country.
We are so far apart.
But I still carry them in my heart.
I still care.

When the darkness comes into my life,
I can still see their eyes, filled of tears.
Remembering some of the inhuman action we did.
We followed orders.
Despite the price.
The price that I lately discover,
When I close my eyes to rest.
I am brought back into those events.
And as it goes, they become vivid.

I brought home demons within me.
I don't want my son to see me angry.
Angry for no reason.

How can I explain why I am like this?
Years ago, the fight was overseas.
Today, the fight still goes on.
Within.

I still feel like I will be attacked.
That my safety is being threatened.
Society sees me as a veteran,

Without any desire to understand.
The weight that each one of us has to carry.
Daily.
Peace has a price.
And I would not change my life.
For my family.
For my brothers and sisters.
I would take selflessly the same path.
We didn't wear a cap. We didn't expect to be recognized.
We gave.
For everyone.
And some gave all.

Today, I don't wear a uniform.
I wear my pride, my injuries, and my demons,
That daily challenge me,
Because I believe in this country.

I am rediscovering how to live...
I once was in a black and white world.
Where a frame surrounded my actions.
I had to have a certain haircut.
Was obliged to timings, rules.

I wore a uniform.
This uniform represented a force,
A way of thinking,
A purpose,
A way of living.

These days, I am learning how to step out of this uniform.

Learning about a world where the colour grey is a way of living.
Where injustice is omnipresent.

Everything I preached for... Was it a dream?

I used to follow this orderly life.
I walk outside and there is little to no direction.
I am remembered daily that the way I see life
Is actually wrong.
People want to fix me.
When truly there is nothing wrong.
With me.

I am wired differently.

OPERATION: WIRED DIFFERENTLY

BRIEFING TWO
OBJECTIVE: BONJOUR READER

Tell Me A Story, I'll Tell You Mine

I've always been encouraged to discover through academic study and art.

At a young age, I loved to read. And the books provided were for much older readers. As a teenager, the writers who interested me the most were Paulo Coelho and C.J. Young. When I look at my lifetime of reading, I might say it has not been strictly for pleasure. Though many say Coelho writes stories, his works are allegorical, their depth a quest into a different level of spirituality—a journey I take seriously. There came to be a rhythm of art in my life, in all its forms. In my teenage years, I wrote over 350 poems.

Early on, I became a fan of history: the stories that built the future. I rounded out my reading with an interest in worldly cultures and traditions, mostly from South America. I learned Spanish when I was a five-year-old—my mother taught me Spanish by playing Scrabble. Later, as a young adult, I was able to experience a youth-exchange in Brazil.

In recent years, the books I read are related to soldiers and PTSD, conspiracies, Nazi projects (medical experiments, special projects, the Fourth Reich) so that I can learn as much as possible about others so that I can apply it to myself and my situation.

Currently, I read to build up my grit, to learn, and grow.

Now, I am writing for that reason too. I didn't see my own book coming—how could I?

I was immersed in protection, consumed with running toward the proverbial burning building, not away from it. It was a call to duty: write or die, write and make a difference. Each day, I make for the computer and pour myself into spaces between the keys on the keyboard. The experience often seems as perilous as any in my military and police careers.

Is my book a story? Perhaps. A narrative, memoir, and message. A work of heart and work of art. A mining of my soul and my psyche. A gesture akin to extending the hand that saves a life.

Together But Apart

Before I was me, born into the life of my parents—two academics—my mother had studied in Colombia, South America, where she learned Spanish; she devoted time to help developing nations. My dad, from a poor family, had travelled North America, hitchhiking the USA, returning via the Westcoast of Canada.

Born in Montréal on July 27, 1986, I was raised in Trois-Rivières, a million miles away from the Canada most know—even all things 80s couldn't bring it closer to the rest of the country. But it was where my Separatist mother (Vive Québec and poutine), and a father who believed in 'live and let others live their life', chose to spend theirs. Dad, a psychologist/sociologist, worked with men who are violent toward family members. Before becoming a mediator for the government, Mom, a psychologist/sexologist with a master's in mediation, worked with female teenagers who had been sexually assaulted by their family members.

Despite the collective breadth of knowledge between my parents, there was a strong family identity as Québecois. My parents did not speak English—I call them true Quebeckers. Though she never told me, I am confident my mother voted for Québec to become its own country. Even today, at the time of writing, they still don't speak English other than the occasional word—which makes it interesting since my wife does not speak French.

At home, I was taught that the English were bad people, historically 'screwing' us (Quebeckers) over and over. Alarmingly, I did not know about Remembrance Day until I was 19; it was not a recognized 'holiday' at home. Apparently, during World War Two, my grandfather hid in the forest so as not to be found to be enlisted; my uncle faked being crazy so as not to complete his bootcamp. Back then, my knowledge of that war was limited, and was shaped by the view of my parents. Now that I have served, I have a different perspective. I don't want to call my grandfather a coward for hiding; I understand I am not in his shoes.

At school, we never learned about the history of Canada; it was the history of Québec and the Nouvelle France. Political classes were taught by a Separatist who sprinkled all exchanges with a hatred toward the Anglo community—English was truly the stuff of the Twilight Zone.

My father worked many hours to pay the bills. During the week, he'd work at the community therapy centre—a subsidized organization—and on the weekends he was employed as a therapist at a prison for youth. My mother worked long hours as well—sometimes she worked outside of Canada. Daycare was deemed too expensive for my parents and so my grandparents took care of me. Their stories of raising my father in poverty were plentiful—they were champions of saying 'things are different now'. Their references to the World War Two, including my grandfather's account of his time as a lumberjack, and how the forest provided him a place to hide rather than join the forces, were often the subjects of the days.

Despite this insular kind of life on planet Trois-Rivières, my parents helped thousands of people—their compassion for others was abundant, as were their ways of helping others heal. Empathy was a part of our daily life, and I have come to realize that I absorbed this lifestyle and a certain mindset which layered over my genetic predispositions. Serve, protect, help, be there for others, example strength, problem solve, trouble shoot… put yourself last after all others.

ABC, 123... A Child In Adult's Soul

I never had many friends—I remember only two. Time was spent with my parents and their colleagues and friends. For this reason, I spoke more like an adult than a child. When there were playground fights, or bullies appeared, I did not have the right tools. Besides, my parents worked against violence; I was told not to confront a bully—I collected a few bruises and lost a lot of fights. Peer rejection featured in my early school years… but that changed in high school.

My parents had the belief that a boy needed a highly structured life; they placed me in a private elementary school. Most private schools in Québec are catholic. I was taught by nuns (sisters); all students wore uniforms, but, unlike the horror stories of the fifties, we were not hit by rulers or punished severely—yet they had authority and we were fearful of them.

When I was nine, I had to adapt and become more independent to help my mother. My sister was born. The same year, my dad was diagnosed with severe depression: burnout. That year was not easy; my dad was suffering alone, my sister was an infant, and my mother had planned for me to change schools because they recognized I had a strong artistic side.

Another private school: all boys, the music teachers were priests. The schedule was grueling as it centred around academics and art. Mornings were study followed by thirty minutes for lunch, then piano. Afternoons were singing—choral. Everything centred around school. For example: Monday nights, I'd arrive home, do my homework, then at six-thirty attend singing practice until nine o'clock. Sundays, along with other students, I sang at morning mass from nine-thirty until noon.

The French Canadian school system differs from the rest of Canada. Grade 1-6 for elementary, and then 1-5 for high school.

High school was boys only, a seminary. Once again, I was in a private school where we had to have good grades to remain. I had difficulty being accepted and to mix myself with others. The first year of five was an international program: French, English, Spanish, plus culture classes, and the regular curriculum including math and science.

During that year our house burned down. To the ground. Perhaps the reason I recall few details is the pragmatic view my parents had: deal with it, move on, find a solution, keep helping others, don't stop working. The house was rebuilt over the summer; we lived at friend's apartment that whole time.

Life became more difficult because we had adjustments to make around the very heart of the family—the home. My parents had massively busy schedules. There must have been upheaval, but I don't seem to have placed the 'event' as anything but a difficult time, including when I got a job delivering newspapers to help out my family.

That first year, despite all the reading I'd done, I failed English class and had to do summer school. It's ironic that now I barely remember how to write in French, and am writing a book in English.

The following year, I asked to be transferred to another private school. I was ashamed of myself for failing the class, and I didn't have many friends. I created a type of self-rejection—I was ashamed because I was not allowed to fail; it weighed on me. When the second year of high school began in a new private school, I went to class in a better state of mind. The new (to me) school had only just changed from an all girls format to a mixed—there were barely any males there—seven boys per classroom. It was fantastic: girls don't beat each other up in the same way that boys do. But mean girls are mean girls, though it was easier on me; they destroyed each other's reputations with a few cruel words. One thing I was able to do was talk—after all, it was what my parents did. It's what I'd learned.

That same year, my mother left to work in Cameroon for two months. Though her working abroad was not new to us, it was still an adjustment given the difficult year we'd had previously.

The remaining high school years were decent; I was a good student. At some point I looked for other activities, and asked my mother if I could join the Army Cadets. My request was denied. The army was a symbol of oppression for my mother; she had been exposed to it coming from the military of Colombia, Cuba, Haiti, and Cameroon when she had travelled the world. Following that, I was enrolled in science camp and poetry groups; sport was not a big thing for me.

To sum up those sixteen years, I openly say I had a well-supported childhood: good examples to follow, loving and supportive parents, positivity at every juncture. The challenging times every family goes through were met with creativity and were framed by the opportunity to grow.

The Ultimatum

At 16 years old, I attended CEGEP (pre-university), my first exposure to public school. I was free and unchallenged; spent more time socializing than studying. Now, at 17, after my first year of pre-university, my father gave me an ultimatum: 24 hours to find a second job or move out. I was already working as a cook in an Italian restaurant. Stubborn by nature, I would be leaving. Within two hours, I had a job interview lined up in Mont-Tremblant, a six hour bus ride away.

CEGEP stands for Collège d'enseignement général et professionnel, which means General and professional teaching college. In Québec , Canada, it is a public school that provides the first level of post-secondary education.

I later discovered my mother did not know about the ultimatum until ten years after my father issued it. It wasn't until recently that I realized my mother built me to achieve and perform. It explains why I ask a lot of myself, and have expectations of myself. It could be said that she was demanding, but I had no reason to believe the way she raised me was wrong. She gave me tools to succeed and to seek bigger challenges. I've also had the opportunity to think about my sister who is eight-and-a-half years younger than me—I hardly knew about her life when I lived at home. I recognize that I had a lot of resentment because I saw her as having stolen my parents. I still believe we were raised differently due to my parents being financially better off when she came along.

A ski resort town, Mont-Tremblant is like Banff, Alberta, but with a small mountain. By mistake (or was it fate or an intervention by faith?) I went to the wrong hotel: the Fairmont. I argued with the lady from human resources, certain I had an interview. I didn't let up. She offered me a 'chef en salle' at their hotel. Though the words translate to kitchen manager, the duties were of a cook. I worked there for six months, then I jumped on another bus to ride across Canada to find work in Banff, Alberta.

I had never been further than Ottawa. I had no idea how big the country was, or how long it would take to get across Ontario, nor how boring the prairies would be, but I went. I barely spoke a word of English.

Independence

In my backpack I had 26 slices of bread, a jar of peanut butter, and 2 litres of water. My chequing account contained $52.00. I remember, on the bus ride, repeating, "I don't speak well, but I understand very well." I was hoping that it would sound good when I said it; truly I didn't understand much. Seventy-two hours of nonstop travel I got out in Canmore, a town close to Banff. I slept on a park bench. I met a friend from back home at a coffee shop, and he offered a place for me to sleep. When I arrived, I found out it would be on the floor with his dogs. Sleeping on the floor was warmer than sleeping on a park bench—there are bears in Canmore. I didn't stay long in Alberta—five months or so, and I still didn't speak English—before flying back to Toronto and bussing back to Montréal. I arrived on December 25th; my father picked me up.

A few weeks later, I received a phone call from Canada Youth World. They offered me the opportunity to be part of a cultural exchange to Brazil. I didn't have much on the go, and accepted the challenge. Sign me up! I'd be living in the country of my favorite writer Paulo Coelho—I read more of his books while I was there.

I went to Brazil with seven other Canadians. My English was only marginally better, and I had to learn Portuguese. We were each paired with a Brazilian—my partner was named Eduardo.

It was amazing to see how their world was different than Canada—Québec life had been so insulated. The danger didn't seem to bother them. We lived in Rosario Do Sul RS, where, as World War Two neared its end, some Schutzstaffel officers fled to.

The program lasted about seven months. Returning home was a shock, especially being back at my parents' home, with rules, curfews and back to their frame. I reconnected with old friends, most of them living in apartments with their girlfriends. I'd been traveling more than two years and seen things that amazed me. I didn't know how I would settle down.

"Train For Your True Calling" (Canadian Armed Forces Recruitment Campaign)

After a few months, I attended the recruiting center of the Canadian Armed Forces. What I did not know then is that recruiters are not human resources specialists with degrees in communication and psychology. To be a recruiter in the military requires a course in Base Borden for a few months. A recruiter doesn't always know the details about the jobs; they will simply direct the prospective soldiers to a computer station so that the enquirer can do their own research.

Quite often, a person will sign up for a job without really knowing what it entails.

The recruiter who dealt with me was an artillery reservist, a Master Corporal.

My first choice was infantry, my second choice was a trade in communication, and lastly intelligence. The recruiter reviewed my application and noticed the languages I spoke, then told me to go the route of Communication Research Operator. The category of this job was labelled 291. The 291's had the opportunity to become translators. This trade required a top-secret clearance and special access. All he could tell me was that it involved translation, but since it required specific security clearance, that I'd be like James Bond.

I was 19-year-old and would believe anything I was told.

Who wouldn't want to be James Bond?

He informed me that after completing my bootcamp I would be on a course of a few months on Base Kingston, then be posted for a few years in Canadian Forces Station Alert. CFS Alert is located in Qikiqtaaluk Region, Nunavut, the northernmost permanently inhabited place in the world. Population of 62, not counting the 215 military members. I didn't think I'd mind that. It would be different. The thing is, I didn't go there. And that is a perfect example of how recruiters don't always know what will happen to a recruit.

The website said that 291 designations would work with extremely sensitive information in a high-security, restricted-access facility. Typically working in shifts, they also have frequent opportunities to work regular business hours and can be deployed around the world.

The reality would be completely different.

This trade was marked as a 'purple' trade, which meant it could be found in the three elements (army, navy and air force). The recruiter asked me to make a choice of which I would join. Each element or branch has its own culture and history, but this is how the recruiter sold it to me:

Do you like to go camping?

He indicated if I did, then the army was for me.

Flash forward: camping in the military is very different than going camping with your family. I was extremely naïve.

Do you like to go on cruises?

This was his pitch for the navy.

From what I have heard, the type of cruise the navy has is nothing like the Carnival Princess with the waterslides and five-star dining rooms

He never talked to me about the air force but, from what I have since learned about the branches in the military, he could have asked me:

Do you like to be in a five star hotel?

And, at that time, when I was 19, if he had asked that, I would have said, 'YES'. I would still say 'YES' now. *I am kidding, my Air Force friends, I love you.*

I went for the army. That is what I had seen in movies… but I'd never really watched military movies (so I guess I assumed), and I never really liked to swim.

SHE NOW SLEEPS BESIDE SOMEONE ELSE

More than a decade ago, I went on a dating website to meet ladies. I believed the dating site a good ice-breaker before meeting in a little coffee shop to see each other and make sure neither is a sociopath.

I have never been great at small talk in bars, always more interested in deeper conversation around coffee or wine.

Rewind to that time: my English was what I would have described as 'rustic' and 'broken'. Clearly it was not what it is today. But in my rustic—maybe I meant rusty—speech, I became comfortable with flirting in English… started to enjoy it. I met my fair share of people; some remained friends and some were flings.

At the end of September 2010, I started to exchange messages, then talk, with a lady from Ottawa. I remember it as if it was yesterday: her profile picture was a selfie in which she wore a Senator's hockey ball cap over her blonde hair; she described herself as active and having a good sense of humour.

I have never been very attracted to blondes, but there was something different with this one. Anyway, I commented about her hat, because it was not the right night to wear it. It was not the Canadien's cap from Montréal. At the time it felt like a clever, smartass comment.

Let me tell you, I do not cheer for any hockey team. My father stopped watching hockey in 1994, when the Nordique of Québec City were moved to Colorado. I attended the Nordique's last game between the Canadiens and the Nordique at the Forum of Montréal. Even though I wasn't a fan of hockey, I had a little bit of knowledge to argue with people and mock them, especially mocking the Maple Leaf fans… but I digress.

The blonde Senator fan and I chatted for a few weeks. Then came the day when she would drive to visit her family in the Toronto area and stop at my house in Kingston for dinner. That would be our first date; I would cook. The menu included fish, asparagus, and a baguette. She would be in charge of bringing the wine.

I remember being hypnotized by her laugh as she tried hard to understand my broken English—I could tell she had a lot of patience. That first night, I told her about my job, that I had some nightmares that haunted my nights, and that I didn't always find it easy.

Before she left my house, words that I never told anyone came to my lips.

"I hope you come back."

The love story was not easy; it took its love-story pages and climbed into the car of a rollercoaster. I was not the only one seeking her heart and she had to make the decision to stay in a love story that she had been comfortable in, or try out something new, something uncertain, something her mother would never advise.

I remember the first time I told her: "I love you." February 13 (our Valentine's day). She answered thank you, and left my house.

Some years later, I asked her what she found interesting in me. She mentioned my pride, being fearless, that I would push through any walls that stand between me and my goal, defeat anything that jeopardized romance.

I had written her a few poems to win her love.

Fast forward to today.

I am hypervigilant when I go out; foresee threats everywhere. I feel only safe at home. I am still filled with pride, but my heart is clouded by a form of sadness.

I have always been in touch with my feelings, but since I removed my uniform my heart speaks louder than my mind. As if, since I had to tame my heart for so many years, I have an overflow of feelings.

I love her more than I ever have. I've offered to cease our relationship. That way she would not be hurt when my heart brings her on a rollercoaster of hardship. Every time I have told her that she should take the easy way out, she has told me to stop, that she is here for good, that it would be the easy path to leave me, but long term she would regret it. She is adapting to this new man, the one who wants to be more artistic, and who wants to create instead of protecting his country.

She now lays beside a different man, one that doubts his choices, his every move. Yet she is still there, she is still adjusting to my craziness and is still a wonderful wife… and marvellous mother. I know that, some nights, she sheds tears when I am not looking at her. She doesn't want me to see her like that. She keeps repeating that I am her rock, when truly she has been mine for years now.

She could have left me. Yet every night she is by my side, believing in us.

I don't know a better way to tell her how thankful I am—that she is here every single day—except to write about her.

I HAVE BEEN LUCKY

I am driving my vehicle on the dirt road, facing the mountains, the sun is watching my every move. My son in my rear-view mirror is looking outside. So young, so pure, he still has no idea of the world he is on. He still believes that spiders and sharks can be his friends, that the darkness is only the world where the shadows live. In the tranquility of the mesmerizing view, I remember my friends who have not had this chance. The ones who never left the battle.

Before taking the road, I set up my playlist named 'soldier on'. A playlist I created to never forget the ones who gave it all. A song comes up, *Fallen Soldier*. The story of man who went to Iraq and, during a patrol, came under fire. Someone was hit. He was hit. Sadly his return to his country is in a pine box… in a coffin. His father was waiting for him. The whole squadron shook the father's hand.

Every time this song has the same effect on me.

This morning, driving away, my son in the back seat, I tear-up looking at him. I used to have nothing to lose, now I have him. It could have been my son who ended up with a Cross of Valour, a flag, and a father he would never know. There is a cost to be a hero and my son would have paid the price for it.

I slow down, park on the side of the road and put my four-ways on. I unbuckle my seat belt, get out of my SUV, open his door and kiss him. He is only two years old and mostly will never remember this moment, but I will. I have been lucky to survive, and pull through. Is it God, an angel, or simply the path I am on?

I won't look for the answer to this question, but I will make sure to love this little man and cherish every moment I have with him.

After the kiss, he smiles and says in his toddler way, "Love you, Daddy."

One more tear runs down my face, a good one. He is the reason why I took this new path, the one where I will give the world to my family. He deserves a father at home, not broken by stress and anxiety. He deserves a father who will be there as he discovers this world.

I sit back in my driver's seat, buckle up and before taking back the road, tell him:

"To you little man, I will always be by your side, never behind, nor up front. As a guide, I will support your quests. I will not give you the answers but fill you with riddles. I will watch you fall and be there to show you how to heal. I will transfer my knowledge via my experiences. I will warn you of the darkness in our souls. You will be stronger that I am because you are like your mother. Someone who has a heart for the whole family. I will hold you in my arms when the storm becomes too much… I might not be a soldier, or a police officer anymore, but forever I will be protecting."

His answer is simple. He points forward and says: "That way."

We take the road and I smile, feeling lucky.

OPERATION: WIRED DIFFERENTLY

BRIEFING THREE
OBJECTIVE: MENTAL HEALTH

Ten Thousand Paper Cuts

To understand PTSD, is to comprehend the combination of rationalization of trauma and the accumulation of it as well. Take a human being—specifically their brain—who has been trained to be anti-flight. They operate effectively within these guidelines… to a point. But there may come a time—either during their service or after they have left—when the events they've experienced—at least some—become, as a collective, incomprehensible and impossible to categorize by the compassionate mind. One papercut is barely noticed. Ten thousand is impossible to ignore.

Civilian Speak

Mental health refers to the level of psychological well-being an individual displays as they emotionally and behaviourally function in a reasonable way. It can also be described as the absence of mental illness. Mental illness, also called mental health disorder, refers to a wide range of conditions that affect a person's mood, thinking, and behaviour. Examples of mental illness include depression, anxiety disorders, schizophrenia, eating disorders, and addictive behaviors.

Operational Stress Injury (OSI)

In the Canadian military, mental health issues are categorized as 'operational stress injury'. Prior to this name, the terms used have included: combat stress reaction, combat fatigue, shell shock, acute stress reaction, battle neurosis.

World War One used the term 'shell shock' to describe psychiatric illness due to injury to the nerves. Sadly, back then—and even now—this kind of injury is perceived as a weakness. For that reason, specific to war, for as long as people have been affected by its trauma, they have also kept it quiet, self-medicated (often with alcohol), and suffered silently.

OSIs are experienced in many situations: active combat, traffic accidents, suicide scenes, and incidents involving children. People have experienced an OSI due to being harassed or receiving a moral injury. Put simply, an OSI is any ongoing psychological difficulty that arises from events related to duties performed. When work-related experiences have a prolonged and significant negative effect on a person's daily life, then certain symptoms can be experienced, observable by those in their family and/or by their co-workers. These negative effects may result in a diagnosis of PTSD, major depressive disorder, anxiety, obsessive compulsive disorder, and/or substance abuse disorder.

Symptoms that are often observed in a victim of OSI are as follow:

- lack of sleep
- anger

- lack of concentration
- numbness (dulled response to life situations)
- isolation
- avoidance
- suicidal thoughts
- racing thoughts
- flashback
- negative view of self
- paranoia

That will impact their life in certain ways:

- difficulty to engage in relationships
- poor work performance
- poor personal care
- poor sleep
- lack of tolerance
- lack of patience
- outburst of aggressivity (rage)
- lack of fear for own life

Responses And Consequences

The brain functions to keep the body-system alive—its first action during a trauma is to go into flight or fight mode, flight being the favourable option for survival. But, in the military, soldiers are trained to fight, therefore when 'fight or flight' mode kicks in, a trained soldier will work hard to overcome their natural instinct of 'flight' (run away).

Living in constant stress impacts the way the brain works.

Traumatic situations can bring about disassociation and loss of memory. Sometimes, the inner-struggle to balance the system can cause certain aspects to shut down. Later, memories and reminders of traumatic events can trigger the brain to re-live the trauma. People affected by trauma will often avoid situations, including social events, as a way to protect themselves.

The stage after avoidance is withdrawing from family, friends, and the society as a whole. Again, this is an attempt to escape or numb any pain related to the traumas. By shutting down the "outside world', there are not as many feelings to be experienced—or so a sufferer believes.

Through numbing by avoiding, people who suffer from traumatic injury lose touch with things that gave them joy: hobbies, music, theatre, exercise. For example, a person who loved to cook and celebrate around food might lose their energy and interest around trying new recipes, even lose their sense of taste (the tastebuds will not send the same messages to the brain).

As much as the victim is affected, family and friends will also suffer. In some situations, family or friends might feel that the person is being lazy or difficult.

Numbing and avoidance can present as:

- loss of memory
- loss of interest in normal activities
- feeling disconnected from the world
- difficulty foreseeing the future

As individuals become consumed by their trauma, they may find themselves confronting their own mortality. Their belief in themselves—that they were stewards of security, tasked to 'save and secure the world'—becomes eroded; a reputation stained.

The concept of 'it will never happen to me' fades. A reality kicks in. There is shame. There is despair. There is a giving up. Now they are the ones to be 'saved' and that is not a role they've trained for. They may have to take leave from their job, resign from work, close down their career—options that go against their original drive to serve. But how? They have not learned or, as in my case, forgotten how to put themselves first; it has always been about others.

Because of the exposure to constant danger in operations, the 'casualty' will now feel or see themselves as being in danger 24/7, even if they have returned home. They will be hyper-aroused, jumpy, irritable, and have angry outbursts within themselves, and against the world. This anger might be demonstrated verbally or physically, which can be very damaging to family and friends. The casualty might experience a sense of betrayal; they have served and are now tossed aside.

The symptoms of hyper-arousal:

- disturbed sleep
- anger
- lack of concentration
- always on the lookout for threats or danger
- jumpy

The Collective Injury

When things do not connect with our moral belief, we work hard to make sense of the situations when, in fact, what is needed is to make peace with them.

Due to the high level of stress associated with severe traumas, the brain will push the event—the memory—aside for a time, registering within the body-mind that the issue has been dealt with. Later, something that reminds the person of the event—a trigger—will surface. Once surfaced, it will keep bobbing like a fishing float under which bait is nibbled by a trout.

Eventually, the fish bites, and takes the float under.

The trigger takes one under the water. It is challenging to be in the present. It is difficult to take care of the self, to go to work, to fall asleep, even to do small chores around the house. Normal routines are impossible to follow when a person is beneath the surface.

In people with PTSD, their threat detection system becomes so sensitive that alarm bells go off even when there is no danger. The person's view of reality is altered. They may only operate in survival mode, as if still at war. During this time, the person might not realize the extent of their trauma-related symptoms, therefore may not understand what is going on within, or comprehend the responses of those around them.

PTSD is often diagnosed in conjunction with other conditions and behavioural disorders such as depression, anxiety, dissociative disorder.

Depression is a general state of low mood and loss of interest, pleasure, and joy, which is sustained over a significant amount of time. Different than situational depression (short periods of feeling sad about something), life becomes 'grey'. Statistics report that 50% of people with chronic PTSD also suffer from depression.

Those with PTSD who are depressed often feel guilt for having survived when others did not. Other times, they may feel ashamed of their previous actions or reactions. Guilt can ensue from having applied the combat training solution to a situation (run toward danger, perform as trained, no flight), thus storing the repressed 'natural' (run away) response.

The nature of war is such that there are often no acceptable or good options: all options are bad (kill or be killed).

Symptoms of depression:

- feeling low, miserable
- feeling worthless
- helplessness
- hopelessness
- lack of joy
- loss of interest
- loss of sexual desire
- loss of appetite
- thoughts of suicide or death
- poor memory, concentration, and decision making

Anxiety, often seen as part of PTSD, is the state of being constantly worried that something will happen.

Symptoms of anxiety:

- fearfulness
- terror
- palpitation
- sweating
- shaking
- fear of losing control
- the sensation of going crazy
- excessive worry
- restlessness
- being on edge
- muscle tension
- tightness in the chest

Statistics show 50% of males and 25% of females with PTSD abuse alcohol and/or drugs, to deal with the symptoms, believing it will help them tolerate ongoing trauma. As a coping strategy, it is a poor one, affecting relationships, work, finances, and health.

Mental Health Management, Strategies, And Solutions

Never underestimate the power of simple approaches that are advocated by numerous professionals.

- Eat healthy meals; a clean diet is proven to lower stress levels.
- Be physically active—walking, jogging, swimming, cycling, weightlifting.
- Get enough rest. If you don't sleep at night, attempt daytime naps.
- Meditation, hypnosis, yoga or like movement modalities will relax your mind and body, which will lower your stress, and reduce anger.
- Establish a routine. It doesn't have to be a full schedule; set up something that you can maintain and be true to. Predictability will help you be accountable and give your brain a kind of balance.
- Set small goals. Gently retrain yourself to show that you can accomplish things.
- Set your priorities.
- Rediscover yourself outside of the uniform. Who are you? Take the opportunity to explore this.

- Join groups. Choose those that reflect your speciality.
- Educate yourself. Read books about mental illness.
- Figure out your limits and respect them—do not push yourself to go beyond them. Be gentle with yourself.
- Acknowledge when you are being triggered. Share with your spouse and family so that everyone has the same information and can understand when focus is needed.

Professionals And Treatment

Professionals and patients agree, finding the right psychologist/social worker with whom you can share your inner-secrets is a massive exercise in trust. Be open to the process of finding the right fit. Welcome therapy. Understand that it will be necessary to find a guide to help you visit the darkest time.

Curate a team so that your mental health professional, counsellors, and other doctors can coordinate their care, including medications.

Family members are team members too. Involve your family to the point you are comfortable with sharing. The process is not without pain, but it is the only way out of the overwhelming symptoms of trauma-related injury. Professionals can offer tools to deal with your day to day and, essentially, offer you a path to a healthy future.

Beyond therapy, there are stabilization groups, which offer more tools and valuable knowledge of mental illness. Group work can help people realize they are not alone; there is an undeniable bond of safety within the group, and a strong sense of caring—that others will check on you, and you on them.

As you move through the healing process, the education you receive in learning about your own condition can help you recognize it in others—another role that is highly valued. As you stabilize, you will learn techniques to manage various aspects of PTSD.

Managing anxiety:

- breathing techniques
- grounding
- method to break intrusive thoughts
- rational self-talk
- relaxation

Anger management:

- identifying early signs of anger
- re-evaluating the situation through perspective
- crisis preparation
- problem solving strategies
- distraction

Depression management:

- positivism
- identifying patterns
- rationalization
- coping self-talk

Cognitive Behavioural Therapy (CBT)

Different therapies work for different people.

In CBT, clients learn to identify, question, and change the thoughts, attitudes, and beliefs related to the emotional and behavioural reactions that cause them difficulty.

By monitoring and recording thoughts during upsetting situations, people learn that how they think can contribute to emotional problems such as depression and anxiety. CBT helps to reduce these emotional problems by teaching clients to: identify distortions in their thinking; see thoughts as ideas about what is going on, rather than as facts; stand back from their thinking to consider situations from different viewpoints.

The CBT model is built on a two-way relationship between thoughts (cognitions) and behaviours. Each can influence the other. There are three levels of **cognition:**

1. Conscious thoughts—rational thoughts and choices made with full awareness.

2. Automatic thoughts—thoughts that flow rapidly—a person may not be fully aware of them. This may mean the person can't check them for accuracy or relevance. In a person with a mental health problem, these thoughts may not be logical.

3. Schemas—core beliefs and personal rules for processing information. Schemas are shaped by influences in childhood and other life experiences.

Behaviour can be changed using techniques such as self-monitoring, activity scheduling (for depression), and exposure and response prevention (for anxiety).

https://www.camh.ca/en/health-info/mental-illness-and-addiction-index/cognitive-behavioural-therapy

Cognitive Processing Therapy (CPT)

Trauma can change the way people think about themselves and the world. They may believe themselves to blame for what happened to them. They might perceive that world is a dangerous place. These kinds of thoughts keep people 'stuck' in their mental illness—they miss out on things that used to be enjoyed. CPT teaches a new way to handle upsetting thoughts. Skills taught in CPT help people decide there are other ways to think about the trauma. This includes ways to examine whether the facts support the person's thoughts (or do not support them). Ultimately, the person can then decide whether or not it makes sense to take a new perspective.

https://www.ptsd.va.gov/understand_tx/cognitive_processing.asp

Eye Movement Desensitization and Reprocessing (EMDR)

EMDR is an evidence-based treatment for post-traumatic stress disorder (PTSD). This means that it has been studied by many researchers and found to be effective in treating PTSD. Most people who complete 1-3 months of weekly 50-90 minute sessions of EMDR show a noticeable improvement in PTSD symptoms; a great number begin to notice improvements after a few sessions.

After trauma, people diagnosed with PTSD often have trouble making sense of what happened to them. EMDR helps people process the trauma. The subject, patient, or client of EMDR is required to pay attention to a back-and-forth movement or sound while calling to mind the upsetting memory. This is done until shifts occur in the way a particular memory is experienced. As the therapy progresses, more information from the past is processed.

Accelerated Resolution Therapy (ART)

ART is an emerging, efficient therapy for PTSD and other psychiatric conditions. It is derived from Eye Movement Desensitization and Reprocessing (EMDR), but has a tighter procedure. ART has been reported to be effective, efficient, and gentle for patients, and straightforward for clinicians to facilitate.

https://www.psychiatrictimes.com/view/accelerated-resolution-therapy-ptsd

Prolonged Exposure Therapy (PET)

When two things appear together, the brain can learn to connect them. This is the premise of PET. Ivan Pavlov created the most famous associative learning experiment by repeatedly ringing a bell before presenting his dogs with food. The dogs began to salivate at the sound of the bell. They had learned to associate the bell with food. To break this association, Pavlov then repeatedly rang the bell without giving the dogs any food. The dogs eventually stopped salivating when they heard the bell.

When trauma occurs, the brain connects certain smells, sights, sounds with that trauma. Then, when a person with PTSD encounters those smells, sights, and sounds again, the person's brain anticipates the same danger—which causes fear and anxiety. By training to 'not' associate stimuli with the trauma, a person's symptoms of PTSD can be alleviated.

https://www.psychologytoday.com/ca/therapy-types/prolonged-exposure-therapy

Statistics from the Government of Canada:
https://www.veterans.gc.ca/eng/about-vac/news-media/facts-figures/8-0

My Wish For The Future

So, as long as we have peacekeepers in war-torn regions, actively engaged soldiers in defence, and the military in offensive positions, no matter how future wars are fought, they will have to deal with PTSD, and society will need to learn how to support those with PTSD. That is surely a form of PEACE we can aim for and achieve within our communities.

The culture we've been used to, in the military, is that you go to bootcamp and you learn, through the chain of command, that pain is temporary and, if you whine, you will be mocked. Training is centred on building endurance and grit. The problem is, if you have a broken bone, or if you come down with pneumonia, you will need to be treated, and that will be obvious. Not so with trauma. It is hidden.

The 'old dogs' who build the 'new soldiers' need to be re-educated to advocate for more openness. They need to explain that it is okay to ask for help. This would be a bold and much needed step forward to open the door to disclosing injuries—so many soldiers are afraid they will lose their careers because of that mentally-ill label, categorized as 'not deployable', having P-cat or T-cat (military health categories). They fear the loss of security clearance if further up the chain of command gets wind of their mental health situation. There is an assumption that if the soldier comes forward there will be consequences.

Often, in a room full of soldiers, you will find many alpha personalities who will never come forward and tell their 'boo-boo'—for fear of sounding weak.

True thought-leaders should favour talking openly about mental health issues. New soldiers need to be taught this so, when they become the leaders of tomorrow, they welcome and understand how to anticipate, prevent, and deal with situations directly related to operational stress.

My concern is that old dogs can't learn new tricks. In that case, the old dogs are negatively affecting the advancement of the health of all soldiers. The stigma needs breaking, but the old dogs keep it alive. If the new generation of soldiers—and first responders—are aware of mental illness, it might stop the stigma. People might start to talk about it more openly.

My own projects include building content for them. I'd like to teach a couple of hours in a bootcamp, police camp, or similar institutional settings. Part of that education would involve giving permission to speak about PTSD—it's a subject that's not talked about enough within the ranks. Questions would be important to the presentation because the best ideas and solutions come from collective conversations.

Young and free…
I could barely grow a mustache, let alone a beard,
A skinny kid who never worked out.
Never done anything other than for myself.
Seeking a purpose, needing a challenge, understood it was time for a vocation,
I attended a building, I believed what was told to me.
Unaware of the darkness living on our planet,
I followed the recommendations of the recruiter.

I signed and initialed an unread contract—just a boy.
Locking myself into an unknown future,
Becoming a servant of the queen,
I trusted life that the decisions would bring me to the right place.

I had learned how to party,
Self centered, I did not care or carry anyone,
Always had disregarded tomorrow,
Embracing the present in an 'it has to be fully lived, now, for me'.

I could barely grow a mustache,
Let alone a beard,
A skinny kid who never worked out.
Never done anything other than for myself.

Something was missing.

Although I had watch and read about war,
It was such a foreign concept.
I would take a path that is so far from the tree of my heritage.

Moving to Canada, leaving my country (vive Le Québec),
Because I was told we were a nation.
Saying "au revoir" to my home.

No one foresaw that exit.
Back then,
My knees didn't hurt.
My heart was at peace with the world.
Life already had a plan for me.
To follow the path of my parents.
Become a professional of the mind—a plethora of degrees under my belt.

Now I am injured, carrying a rucksack of nightmares,
And I say, if I could have seen the future.

And I know, I would still have taken the path I took.

It was in the uniform that I discovered who I am.
In the hardship and pain, I pushed my limits.
In learning the truth,
I equipped myself with knowledge not known by most people.

I found love; my son was the result of it.

In that naïve state,
When I was a skinny kid,
Who could barely grow a mustache,
Let alone a beard,
I made the right choice.

When I was more than yesterday young…
Sitting in the passenger seat of my father's 1999 Saturn,
Almost a soldier,
My father drove me 172 kilometres to the garrison to begin a life,
Neither he nor my mother wished for me.

We turned into the driveway,
Pulled up at the doors to the garrison,
And he looked me in the eyes,
His boy,
Almost a soldier,
His child,
His only son.
Almost a soldier.

"Est-ce que tu veux que je vienne avec toi?"
(Do you want me to go with you?)

"Non, papa."

OPERATION: WIRED DIFFERENTLY

BRIEFING FOUR
OBJECTIVE: A CANADIAN MILITARY PRIMER

If you know the history of the Canadian Armed Forces proceed to the next briefing!

Do not pass go…

The Types

The Canadian Military has two type of forces: a regular force and a reserve force.

The regular force is exampled as people who sign contracts—different kinds—and become full-time officers of the military. It is their career; they are salaried and receive promotions and develop their careers in a similar way to civilians.

The Reserve Force is a little more complex. An integral part of the forces, reservists come from all walks of life and are called citizen soldiers. Though primarily part-time service, reservists can volunteer for full-time employment.

There are four sub-groups within the Reserve Force:

- Primary Reserve is the largest component; reservists train regularly on a part time basis with occasional periods of full-time service.
- Cadet Organization Administration and Training Services (COATS) is a component which supervises, administers, and trains cadets and Canadian junior rangers.
- Canadian rangers provide a military presence in isolated areas of Canada such as sparsely settled northern and coastal regions. They also support Canadian junior rangers (aged 12-18 in those communities).
- Supplementary Reserve members with past service who are not required to undertake military training except under conditions of national emergency.

Reservists can receive compensation, depending on the level of service and duties.

History

On Feb 1, 1968—the Royal Navy, Canadian Army, and Royal Air Force joined under one identity called The Canadian Forces.

Prior to the unification of the army, navy, and air force, the military drew on the colonial militias—these dated back to the earliest European settlements in North America. Generations before Canada's confederation in 1867, Canada was served by British and French military units. Over time, European powers were reluctant to fund a large standing army in Canada. As Canada opened up, with settlers moving across Lower and Upper Canada and the Prairies, small community-based companies of soldiers—local men and veterans of previous wars who had been granted Canadian land—were established to protect these areas.

The Canadian Navy, whose motto translates as 'from sea unto sea,' protects the longest coastline of any country, but was not formed until May 4, 1910—more than 40 years after modern Canada was created (July 1, 1867). It was completely ill-equipped when Europe descended into war in the summer of 1914.

The Royal Canadian Air Force was formed in 1920, with a royal sanction, by King George V, in 1924. As part of the unification of the Canadian Forces in 1969, air units were split between several different commands: Air Defence Command (interceptors), Air Transport Command (search and rescue), Mobile Command (tactical fighters, helicopters), Maritime Command (anti-submarine warfare, maritime patrol), and Training Command.

Some trades in the military are specific to individual elements while others can be found in every element. That is the case with the one I chose: communication. Those occupations and careers typically related to logistics and support that are present in all three elements—Navy, Air Force, Army—are referred to as purple trades.

The Canadian Armed Forces has Special Operation Force Command which contains five units. People posted to CANSOF go through a series of tests (fitness, psychological, writing, and interviews). Members, other than operators, are usually landed to the SOF community, which means that those people will return eventually to the 'element' they originally signed with. CANSOF units operate around the world, and within Canada.

The first SOF unit officially created in Canada, JTF2, was established in 1993 with members from the RCMP and the military. Their missions are kept outside of the media and general public. The other four units have their own specializations and also operate inside and outside of Canada.

Avenues For Members

During the career of a military member they will go though multiple training programs, some related to their trade, and some to progression if promoted. Depending on the trade that the member opted for, specialization can be a route/option that is taken. The member will be posted within Canada or abroad—this is not deployment but more like an assignment.

Postings come about every four to seven years. For the Navy, those postings can be a move from one coast to the other. If in the Army, their main bases are in Alberta, Ontario, and Québec. Postings abroad can be to an embassy anywhere in the world, or to ally bases. Postings come with myriad logistics, as the member's family is also moved; if children are involved, they require school, perhaps daycare if the spouse is planning to find a new job. House hunting will happen over a short time, a few months prior to the posting.

Historical Perspective

Civilians within and outside Canada mostly think the country is a peaceful place with its military participation in peacekeeping. There have been armed actions over hundreds of years of Canadian history with many battles involving Canadian soldiers.

In 1534, Jacques Cartier planted the flag of France (in what is now Canada/St. Lawrence/East Coast/Québec), laying the base for French claims and initiating inter-tribal conflicts. For hundreds of years, Canada was involved in territorial armed actions. This includes four colonial wars and two additional wars in Nova Scotia and Acadia between New France and New England. Those battles took place within a period of seventy years, and each group was allied with various Indigenous groups.

After the final colonial war—the Seven Years' War—in 1763, the British claimed victory and expected the French civilians to assimilate. In 1774 the Québec Act passed which gave Canadians their first charter of rights under the new regime. The Northern colonies then chose not to join the American Revolution and remained loyal to Britain. After this, the Americans launched invasions in 1775 and 1812. Both times the Canadians were victorious, but the threat remained well into the 19th century.

Controversy followed Confederation. By 1867, a fully operational Canadian military had been created. Canada joined their British counterparts in the Second Boer War and World War One. Canada supported the British (after the Statute of Westminster when Canada gained independence) through the Second World War. Since then Canada has served within multinational coalitions that formed for conflicts such as the Korean War, the Gulf War, and the Afghan War. Canada is also renowned for its peacekeeping role throughout the world.

OPERATION: WIRED DIFFERENTLY

BRIEFING FIVE
OBJECTIVE: WHO JOINS THE MILITARY?

There are families for whom serving in the military is their tradition. They foster the importance of serving their country. For this reason, many members of these families see entry into the military as a right of passage and a way to honour those who went before them. I served with fellow brothers who joined the military because they wanted to follow in their family's footsteps, or felt forced to join because other family members had served.

The value of service to country is not limited to long-standing military families. Many people join to show loyalty to their country. Quite often, people have more than one reason to join. Some people are looking for a purpose and believe the military will help them find it. Others look to the military to obtain a trade or vocation; the military is known for providing skill training in return for service time.

Some recruits believe that they will travel with the military—see the world via their career. Other times, in depressed areas where there are few jobs, the military is seen as a good choice to obtain employment and leave the 'hometown'. Another popular belief by some is that it will be a place to get into shape—quite often this is not the reality. We used to say 'we' are the fittest drunks. But, certainly, the physical demands of the bootcamp and daily workouts require a strong mind and physical aptitude.

There are some people who wish to challenge themselves and see the military as the ultimate physical and mental test.

Learning To Be A Soldier

Once a person has made their choice to join the military, regardless of which element or trade, they will be re-wired. They will be taught to live from 'A to Z'. It is not that people don't know how to live, or their parents didn't do a good job of raising them, it is a matter of needing to be re-wired in order for everyone to be the same. If the base or root of the group is identical, then it is easier to ensure compliancy; easier (and safer) to predict outcomes. It is necessary for the smooth functioning of a massive organization.

If everyone learns how to answer fully to every command then there will be more successful outcomes in the life-saving department. If everyone makes their bed the same way they will also complete every task and follow every order with the same unified military precision. They will fight (not turn to flight) with the same determination and goals. A whole group with a single mindset.

Basically, the mold of the individual has to be broken to create a new casing that casts each as a militarized member. That is what training does.

The military teaches people to work hard, endure suffering, and be proud of achievements… without asking for recognition. There becomes a pride in the uniform which represents country. Yes, each soldier wears their country on their sleeve, right beside their heart.

The military teaches that there is no such thing as 'I'. It is a 'we' that is required in order to attain collective success.

Training is key. Military exercises are done because training leads to perfection. There is always a plan. The military never goes blindly into a situation. In wartime, planning is essential. In peace-time… there is, in a way, no peace-time as the military is always working, behind the scenes, to deal with threats, to evaluate risk, to assess the nation's vulnerability. There is no such thing as 'winging it'.

Many people who join the military understand planning. From logistics in transportation to diplomatic negotiations, the military is filled with planners and soldiers who carry out plans. Those who find their careers in the service face multiple challenges and have the opportunity to problem solve—in life or death situations. The rewards are great for those whose values become aligned closely with the military. Core values are learned: integrity, courage, loyalty, respect, and dignity.

Beyond The Hardship – My Experience

Did I have fun during my service? Do I have great memories?

It is interesting how one can build strong relationships in hardship. I built some of the most wonderful friendships in the military. My tribe are friends and colleagues I've worked and studied with, and deployed alongside. Side-by-side we endured hardships, kept a sense of humour in the most difficult times, and forged unbreakable bonds—we can go without seeing each other for years and pick up where we left off.

My first summer in the military, I was tasked at the naval recruit school which is a reserve school in Borden, Ontario. I was part of the enemy forces—this means I was on the team that tests recruits when they are in their field phase. A small team, we carried out multiple scenarios based on the curriculum for basic military qualifications. These courses would be 20-22 hours a day for 2-3 weeks at a time. Even as I write this, I can hear people saying that this is not healthy. What is necessary to understand is that, through these exercises, people get to see their true selves. We had things to complete and we accomplished them despite the lack of sleep, food, and hygiene. The military exercises I participated in were essential for my success when I was in real-life situations—the enemy does not keep a 9-5, Monday to Friday, schedule. All forces have to be ready to respond at all times.

I take myself back to being screamed at while doing physical training; it was part of the deal and we were pushing ourselves to the maximum of our ability, despite our bodies hurting. Through this I developed a pride I didn't know I had. Later, when training others, I saw this pride develop in young recruits.

During that time, I was one of two French Canadians on the team. Since our names were too complicated to pronounce, we were given nicknames: Archy and Frenchie. We were a hell of a duo—different in our way of thinking, yet I found a friendship like I never had before. Later, we were posted to different bases, and we had separate trades, but we kept in contact. He was the best man at my wedding.

I could tell you that I had fun digging trenches, when truly there is nothing enjoyable about that but, because of those relationships, all the exercises and experiences related to the military were great ones.

Fast Forward

On the strength of relationships and that unified mindset, fast forward to a comparison of my time spent serving in the city police (after the military). I'd say it wasn't as much fun—that the relationships were not as deep. Policing a civilian world is not as much about teamwork as it is about self-drive to reach a higher rank.

This 'rise above the rest' is part of the culture in that negative examples (against fellow officers) are used to receive promotion. This is the polite way of saying there is backstabbing of other officers (over their mistakes) in order to move ahead. It would be much better to have an atmosphere of camaraderie which would help make everyone a better officer.

Of course, I did build some incredible relationships among many officers I served with. Those relationships helped me develop coping skills during the kinds of circumstances the police deal with on a daily basis—heartbreaking, tragic, violent, disturbing, criminal. Humour—a dark humour—is a key to handling the nature of many calls.

In such a dark world, one has to wear a smile to see the sun come out.

There is a selfless type of personality that calls people to enlist. Sadly, not many Canadians understand this drive or motive. A great majority of the civilian population does not realize what is sacrificed for peace, nor do they recognize the gift that soldiers provide.

Take the recruit at the beginning of their service. Firstly, they leave home and move to a base that can be a great distance from where they live. Then they will be expected to quickly adapt to a new set of values—totally different than those they are used to.

Maybe they didn't know it would be so drastic. But they are 'in' now.

Maybe they knew they needed that contrast.

Maybe they didn't know that they were wired differently.

Joe Canada

The typical routine of Joe Canada is 8-5, Monday to Friday with a promotion or two within the same company over twenty-five or thirty years of service.

Jo Student's typical day isn't that much different. Classes in the day, some studies, a party or two on the weekend.

Whether in a civilian job or as a student, Joe Canada operates from a 'safe place'. Their 'own' safe place.

In the military, a soldier on 'course' is studying their trade and has additional responsibilities including regular physical training (PT) and building inspection (cleaning their quarters). Nothing is private: meals are eaten at the mess (cafeteria). If an individual doesn't like the catering, they will need to find the time and money to obtain other food—and locate a place to purchase it—good luck, as every minute of every day is monitored and there is no extra time. There is no 'safe place' anymore. They have left home. Family is elsewhere. The military is family now.

The best way to explain this 'other world' is to emphasize that the military has its own convenience stores, gas stations, (some places even have their own grocery stores), barbers, banks, dentists, eye doctor, hospitals, psychologists, churches, schools, daycares, airports, police (including the laws and code and court system, jail). The 'base' is a world, and even off base can still be branches of that world. For example: the offices of Veterans Affairs.

There are exceptions to this 'full time schedule' which are anomalies that I did experience—more on that later.

Is it any different from a civilian going abroad to study? Of course it is. The student abroad has the freedom to leave at any time, change subjects, return home, have unsupervised time, enjoy unrestricted (undisciplined) leisure time, and be 'individual'. They are not 'on call' 24/7—their 'mold' is not broken.

In comparison, a new recruit signs up for a period of time: 3-4-5 or 6 years depending on the trade they chose. For the time of that contract the soldier belongs to the Crown. To Canada. They will have to follow orders and military law. That means being on time and doing what is demanded of them whether they want to or not.

Yes, Sir. Yes, Ma'am

If the chain of command says tomorrow 'you' are off to be trained, or that you are going on a house hunting trip, this is where you go. You don't have the choice. If you are sick, you don't call from home and tell your supervisor that you don't feel well. You have to go to the MIR (medical inspection room = military hospital). You will require a doctor's note that say that you are going to be off. Before you get that time off, you will have to deliver the note to your chain of command.

Postings will take place. You will be working from a base, and then an order will come through. At that time, it doesn't matter if your kids are settled in a certain school, or your spouse has a stable job.

Beyond that, you are paid per year. That means that on the first and the fifteenth of the month you will receive a salary, which will always be the same. It doesn't matter if you worked an 80 hour week—and you didn't sleep—your pay will not change. Your pay may change if you are deployed abroad and the level of danger is a higher rating than where you were previously. Truly, they might give you a thousand more per month and a tax break.

Is your life's value five thousand dollars?

Sacrifice

This is not a career done for the money. This is done for the bigger picture. Military members sacrifice not being home so that their children and the children of others are in a safer world. They hunt the wolf so that the wolf doesn't hunt their family or the family of others.

There are nations that believe oppression is how to control a population; there are dictators in this world. There are a million complex pieces that fit together behind the scenes that ensure Canada remains at peace—safe from terrorism, strategically protected within treaties within agreements within contracts that boggle the mind. Canada is not 'actively at war' because of actions and decisions that are taken every day by a constantly vigilant military organization. Because of the unified nature of the military, even the recruit on their first day is an integral part of every Canadian's peaceful existence.

FREEDOM. IS. NOT. FREE.

A note on civilian first responders: yes, these are people who are also sacrificing. They wear a uniform too. But there is a difference between this and the military. There is still the option to say no. I've seen some first responders ignore a call, refuse to attend—it is an option. There is a punch-card mentality about it with a start and end to the shift. And while it is a tremendously difficult job to do, it is not the military where there is only one choice: obey.

My Experience

Who was I for so many years? I was a military member. I was in the army. I was the uniform. It was impossible to take it off. There was no such person as Jonathan… When you can only obey, you (as a person) remove yourself from the equation of regular life (and choice). Your entire life becomes the military.

OPERATION: WIRED DIFFERENTLY

BRIEFING SIX
OBEJCTIVE: DON'T WALK ON THE QUEEN'S GRASS

This chapter reflects the system at the time of my entry into the military.

Before even thinking of bootcamp, a person needs to be selected and hired. There is a specific process for that. Everyone who applies to be part of the military goes through a few stages.

Stage one is the application phase: the applicant completes the application; there will be a personnel screening, consent and authorization form. Reference letters are required.

Stage two is the aptitude test which determines abilities including verbal skills, spatial ability and problem solving.

Stage three is the medical test (exam) which is thorough and includes basic tests for heart rate, blood pressure, cholesterol level, and screenings from a urine sample.

Stage four is the fitness test. It is basic endurance, aerobic, and muscle strength.

Stage five is a reliability check—aka a background check to see if there are criminal charges past or pending.

Finally, there is an interview.

Each stage includes the possibility of a fail that either defers the applicant, or prevents enlistment for life.

Bootcamp – Your New World

The clock stops and restarts with a new relationship to the world and to measuring time. No more four o'clock, it's 1600 hours. Or just 'sixteen hundred'. Don't ever forget it, Sir.

The first step when you join the military is the Basic Military Qualification, commonly called Bootcamp, and is usually a mix of the three elements (air, navy, army).

Regular forces (full time military members) will most likely be sent to St-Jean sur Richelieu (Qc), at the Garrison St-Jean. This is your first culture shock. There might be a new recruit class starting every week of the year. You are assigned to a Cadre of instructors (a body of instructors) and you will have a platoon. Each platoon has a different name, for example 0298F; the letter at the end of your platoon is to explain if you are on a French or English course.

To make sure that everyone knows who you are, you will sew your nametag and last three digits of your service number onto your uniform. There will also be identification as to which week you have accomplished, the last week being F, for final.

F for French. F for Final. FF for Fucking Finished.

The first week, you are learning the ranking, filling in tons of paperwork related to administration. Your service number will become a part of you—one letter with eight numbers—as important, or more, than your SIN. You will memorize it and it will follow you throughout your military career. There will be a fitness test; if you fail you will removed from the group you are currently with and be sent to a fitness platoon commonly known as 'fat camp'.

The first week you learn what a platoon senior is. It is a position of leadership within the group—a representative of the class. Generally, the platoon senior will fill the position for a few days; it's a rotating position—everyone will have a turn. Among other duties, the platoon senior reports to the Cadre every morning, stands by the door at the beginning of class, and calls the class to attention when the teacher enters.

The Cadre will set the standard for your cubicle and, in case you forget how it is supposed to be, there are pictures illustrating how it is required to be. Your cubicle constitutes a mattress on a metal bed, a small closet with a few shelves, and a desk. It will all be inspected. Things will be measured and cleaned to an extreme. Every cubicle will be exactly the same.

You are allowed to be up at 0500 and the lights have to be off (you're in bed) at 2300; a staff member will walk through to make sure everyone is following the rules. These are the official rules, but there are not enough hours in the working and waking day for everything to be done. It's not usual for a number of headlamps to illuminate the night as a group does its chores. In the military you can do whatever you want… as long as you don't get caught.

There's the law and on top of it there's the military, and when you go the extra mile to get shit done you can't get caught. Our leaders, they must have known we were doing it. They must have. They had to have done it themselves in their day. They must have found time in the night and applied shortcuts too: you can wash the floor with a mop but if you use the soles of your mucklucks and a bottle of Pledge® it is faster and looks better.

Before I forget, you will learn the military alphabet—known as the NATO alphabet. Instructors get new soldiers to learn it by making them spell their last names—if you have a long last name like mine, 18 letters, they have a lot of fun with you.

When I did my bootcamp, I had a flip phone (cellphone) which the military locked up—we were not allowed access to them. As well, even though there were elevators in the building, recruits were not allowed to use them. If you are on the 8th floor, you learn how to run up and down the stairs. In my platoon, each dorm had 30 beds. There were 60 males and 8 females. The ladies were on the 10th floor.

You learn to do everything efficiently. Showers are fast—no one is allowed to skip shower time (staff check that your towels are damp). In each dorm there were 10 showers, which have to be cleaned and dried. Fifteen of us used one shower and timed each other. No joke, we had someone responsible for timing—no more than 25 seconds each. Recruits cannot make up time by missing meals either. The Cadre ensures that your card has been swiped at the mess (cafeteria).

The first class starts at 0700, unless you have an inspection of your quarters. Classes usually go until 1800, unless you are in trouble. Classes will vary: physical fitness, history, culture, direction and firearms, drills.

At week five, after the platoon succeeds their military march and receives the cornflake, the fundamentals of firearms are taught. This includes how to assemble your firearm in the light and in the dark, as well as all the issues that can occur during use.

Everywhere you go as a platoon you will military march. And everyone will military match—meaning look the same; at certain times it is scheduled for everyone (women exempted) to have their head shaved. March and match. The platoon senior will be the one directing you. There is often an earlier PT class with the Cadre at 0510. Which is never after 0510. We always show up early for all events, even the perceived mundane… there is no room for error in the military. The staff show up on the scheduled time. Precision is everything—in battle you have to be there for the event, not a latecomer. Latecomers miss the boat. They miss everything. Latecomers die. Bald and sleep-deprived, we march as one, ready for the 0510 assignment which will be a run or whatever the superior's imagination can conjure. During the run, just like in the movies, you'll be singing the military song.

Ouhh Ha!

The first week is a lot to take and, if you are the type of person who falls asleep during a PowerPoint® presentation, you will have to stand up. The classes are held in a place like an auditorium; the floor is concrete and that 'standing up for punishment' can really hurt if you are on the stairs and fall asleep again (while standing).

Highlights of various weeks include week five where you are tested on your drill and military march. If you pass, you will receive your 'cornflake' which is the CAF symbol that you can put on your beret. That will also let you access firearms training. As the weeks progress they are more exciting, but more brutal. Week five is the week where you can potentially go out. If your platoon is not a screw up and your Cadre feels you are deserving they will allow you to leave the garrison. I have witnessed some platoons confined to barracks (CB) for the first seven weeks.

I recall how we were taught to make our bed, how to clean our boots, and how to set up our weapons. Everything was done in an orderly fashion and held meaning and deep purpose—we were being militarized. We didn't ask questions for fear or out of respect for authority. I can tell you that I was in the fearful part of the group. There was something in the eyes of those leaders that always scared me. They had been militarized—the empathy was gone.

During the first five weeks—when not in class—you have access to your dorm and the smoke pit. Nowhere else. I thought I was going to stop smoking when I joined the military. I was wrong.

The result of spending day and night with your platoon is that friendships will form. Some of those bonds will be long-lasting. There will be people who break down and some who quit. Some will realize it isn't for them. Others, who might be injured, might be re-classed if the injury is too severe to continue in that part of the training—they will be sent to other classes. On that note, that's why there are sometimes recruits new to a group who have previously been injured and are now able to participate.

Throughout your recruitment course you are competing with your sister platoon, which is either English or French.

The first time you go into the field is week eight. This is where you learn basic duty at a camp, and other infantry concepts. You will not sleep; well, not much. I remember going to the bathroom and falling asleep on a roll of toilet paper; you learn to fall asleep anywhere.

I remember bayonet training. It was a winter's day, so the course took place inside. We were formed into a squadron but with a fair amount of distance between each other. We were instructed how to move and told to scream 'kill' every time we did the movement. It was physically tiring, and extremely repetitive. At the end of that course I had learned how to stab someone by using a knife at the end of my rifle.

There was a time when we were shown film clips that had been recorded by the Taliban. It showed their kills—the victims were Canadians and allies. The films exampled their use of bombs and IEDs. I remember right after that morning feeling such anger that I had it in me to kill every one of those motherfuckers.

I recognize today that I needed that anger. It gave me a form of positive energy; pushed me to become more prepared. I have never been a big guy—I'm not tall—therefore this aggressiveness and anger gave me the power to get stronger, faster, and work towards my strengths.

Learning To Be Invisible – The Grey Man

Military leaders do not see you—not as one individual. The very success of missions, battles, wars, projects are based on unity. A unified group such as a patrol, a platoon, or a student body in a classroom, is just that. A collective with one goal. One view. A joint perspective. A soldier unit.

During bootcamp, you learn quickly that it is better to deal with your issues at the lowest level, meaning the less your Cadre knows the better because, if one person screws up in your platoon everyone does, and that might cost you your weekend.

For example: inspection can happen at anytime of the day. I remember coming back to our dorm and the entire place had been turned upside down. My mattress was in the shower; some guys had shaving cream all over their items. Obviously, there was a crease in someone's bed or some other infraction had been committed by one of us. We all paid the price. There were times, when a recruit forgot to lock their locker and returned to a mannequin made with all their clothing.

Whatever the offence, you have to clean the whole mess, complete your studies, and still be in bed at 2300.

Oh, and about the grass, the Queen's grass… don't you dare walk on the grass because a supervisor or staff will scream at you.

It is a tough course, but you learn to have fun in very hard moments. I have great memories from my course.

There is no more 'me'. Like I said before, if someone doesn't pull their weight, the problem is brought up at the lowest level. If that 'entity' doesn't listen, there will be consequences. A soap party might be arranged (Google it). Some would call it barbaric. Some would call it teaching a lesson. Either way, the whole group has to function as one because, in the field, that means life or death.

GREATER PURPOSE

I was a man of no countries. Nothing was holding me or stopping me. I didn't have any fixed frame, nor fixed address. Signing for the military moved me toward a greater purpose—it was the path I needed to follow. The military culture: yelling, orders, and learning, instilled in me something I'd never had before. It became obvious that structure was being implanted in my life. Through that, I found something that had always been in me: a desire to serve. I discovered that I was selfless and ready to dedicate a great part of my life to others.

When I look back, it is not surprising that I was attracted by this path. I had witnessed my parents helping others throughout my youth. I had observed both of my parents working to exhaustion. Interestingly enough, my sister, nine years younger, ended up in a field where she also helps society.

To be sworn in, right hand on the bible, at first didn't mean much, but I quickly realized what it was bringing to my life. As a military member you don't decide where you end up, or what you will go to war for. You trust your chain of command to do the best for you and the country. I would be lying if I said that I always agreed with what I was ordered to do, or concurred with the decisions that were made at a political level. But it was not my place to fight it, because fighting it would not have been tolerated. It would have been seen as mutiny. Mutiny results in court martial, which nobody wants.

I stood before the flag like many Canadians.

I shaved my head like all those other young men…
Hand on the bible, with god, I was sworn in.
From the east to the west coast,
I became one of those men who would protect our country.

I was adopted by this family,
My DNA was modified, my perspective of the world changed.
My love for our country grew.
Maple leaf on my heart, I learned so much.

In tears, muscles soreness, smiles and unity,
my brothers and sisters discovered why I was me.

This brotherhood understood me,
We were men, soldiers, untouchable,
Yet, those men always had a shoulder for me to fall on.
We were solid, yet still human with sadness and solitude.

I called them family,
As much as my memory is not always great.
I do remember everything with them.
From the run, the trench, the sleep, the training.
Those who were older and had been exposed to more,
Became bigger brothers and sisters to look up to.
They were the example to follow.

I learned to lead, because I had such great examples.
I was re-wired, to a greater purpose,
For our country, that we love so much.

Signing the first contract, years past,
I signed 25 years.
Without knowing where it would bring me to.
Faith in my pockets, I did not question it.

It is a love relationship, a work relationship.
It is part of me, part of my story.
It was not always about fame,
Hell we were not in for the recognition.

We were, are in for you.

After Bootcamp

If bootcamp has not killed you, you are posted to a school base... your school base. For example: communication—CFB Kingston; Royal Canadian Regiment—CFB Petawawa; Medic—CFB Borden.

During training, the courses take place similar to a technical college. Classes and hands on experience. Some of that hands on experience takes place in the field, at other locations, as you are doing on the job training. Like a practicum.

No matter what, the first five years you are being trained in your element. Navy has its own course on a ship. Army has its own land course—physical and book work. Air Force has a specific history course.

An issue that comes up in Canada is that, at times, there are not enough instructors for the amount of recruits that are present. This results in a wait-time for courses. It can be the catalyst for people to leave or to change their choice of specialization.

Post Recruit Education And Training Centre—PRETC

After bootcamp, when every soldier is ready for training in their trade—that trade they picked when they signed up—they take a deep breath, cross their fingers, and hope that there is room. Training spots are not always 'ready and available' for each person; there might be a waiting list, as some positions are highly coveted and have long waiting lists. The English classes that teach trades outnumber the French, so a French soldier may wait longer, or there may be other circumstances.

In the 00s, there was so much hiring going on because of the possible engagement in Afghanistan that there was a glut of graduates, yet insufficient post-bootcamp classes to answer all the trade requests. In this case, when the training spots are not available, a soldier goes into a work situation, pre-training for their trade—waiting for their training for their trade—and that is called PRETC. There is still work to be done, but the tasks are not always related to the trade the person chose. For example, because I chose communication and required a certain security clearance, I could not job shadow anyone doing that job until I had the clearance, whereas an individual to be trained as a mechanic would likely find their tasks related to their trade, including working alongside another mechanic (prior to the trade being taught).

PRETC is basically a platoon of 'waiting soldiers' on hold for a base that will provide the training for their trade.

The tasks vary. They can be helping in training recruits or putting armoured plates on a vehicle.

A task could be for a day, a month, or even a year. I held various tasks including working at the military museum, cataloguing uniforms from World War Two. That job spread over quite a lot of time, whereas I recall using a stick to search for mines in a field—a one day task.

One of the issues within PRETC was that some members became bored. In those cases, soldiers have taken 'time' into their own hands and 'left the base'. Yes, this is a violation that could be court martialed but it happened. Those people who chose to leave, as in 'skip PRETC' and spend time at home rather than doing tasks, did get away with it and got paid for not being there. While I believe it was a symptom of the backlog of people within the system at that time, I am confident that the military has fixed this issue.

The way it happened was that role call was taken in a way that was meant to get through four hundred people with only a 'here' as an answer. We were a crowded base, many of us staying in a building that had been condemned due to asbestos issues. I waited three years for my training. I fully enjoyed most of it and rarely had a day off. When there was no task for me, I'd take a course. I was always active. For others it was not the same. Some became depressed, others got into drugs and alcohol, *some took their own lives*—yes, before they got to be trained and in service—because of the long wait. Within that frustration that some felt, from 1994-2005 there was a salary freeze. All those years, and no increase in pay—these things can be demoralizing and, for some, created the absenteeism that took place in PRETC.

There is a massive positive to PRETC. For me, I had time to expand my mind and skills, visit different aspects of military life—like the museum and looking for mines. My time in all parts of the military was deeply rewarding. My issues arrived only after the military—because there is one thing the training does not do—maybe it cannot do—and that is to prepare soldiers to remove their uniform.

After You Have Your Trade

When you are qualified within your trade, the military will ask you to select three places where you would like to serve. Based on the military's need, and your choices, you will be posted.

You don't always get where you want. I have a friend who had a house with his family in Halifax, NS and was posted to Victoria, BC.

I have been posted to five different locations in twelve years.

When you google 'how many military bases does Canada have?' the number 26 comes up. But don't let that fool you. Besides bases, you can be posted to reserve units, embassies, recruitment centres, ships, undisclosed buildings… Generally, you will be posted every three years or, if you are on a base, you might be posted to a different unit on the same base. Therefore there is a possibility that you might be at the same location for years.

Snapshot Of My Experience – CFB Borden

After bootcamp, as a member of the regular forces, I was posted to CFB Borden.

I soon got used to a routine of marching from our barracks to the area of roll call—a fifteen minute march. We formed up fifteen minutes early, in three ranks.

Then the senior of the platoon would call everyone to attention. Our sergeant would arrive and take roll call. It was not a great system. I know some recruits were covered by others. After the roll call was completed, the CoC would tell smokers to go for a 'butt', and the non-smokers would be sent on tasks—the smokers would most likely do nothing for the rest of the day.

For those without tasks, they only had to show up at roll call early morning, before lunch, after lunch, and at the end of the day. As mentioned, there were some that were simply absent, had gone 'home', and still pulled a salary—troubled souls who were tired of waiting to be sent for their training in their trade. This was completely different than the accountability at Bootcamp.

There were two platoons, one of which would be trained in Borden (logistics, vehicle tech, ammunition tech, military police, medics and others). The other which would be trained on Base Kingston (any trade related to communications and intelligence). In total we were about 400 people waiting for assignment, and while waiting we were doing tasks—some that could be considered on-the-job training, and other work that was unrelated to our chosen field.

While at CFB Borden, I was part of a group tasked to build camp in the field for the recruits' field training. We also had to dig some trenches for some scenarios. It was a warm day, the sun was over our heads. I still remember our sergeant dropping us off in the middle of a field, pointing to the location where he wanted his trenches and telling us when he would come back to pick us up. We were left there with some water and shovels.

When we were close to five feet deep, we found some empty bullet casings—close to one hundred rounds. On the bottom of the rounds was engraved the year 1943.

At the end of the day, I made my own research on 1943 base Borden. The history says that, at first, the base was only a camp, built in 1916 (during World War One). It was named after Sir Frederick William Borden, a former minister of militia. During World War Two, it became the most important training facility in Canada. The British Commonwealth Air Training Plan's (BCAPT) No. 1 Service Flying Training School was located at Borden until 1946.

Is it true? I was told that a Nazi soldier was captured on that base. Knowing that the truth is not always released to the public… I've always wondered about that.

OPERATION: WIRED DIFFERENTLY

BRIEFING SEVEN
OBJECTIVE: OVERSEAS

When I was young, I learned to find beauty in the smallest of things.

It helped me when I needed to ride out challenges in my life. This was particularly useful in the military when I was in the field, sleeping outside, with no safe place to be.

Initially, in 2007, I put my name in a pool of not-fully-qualified soldiers to go to Afghanistan, basically to wash dishes. I had served about five months at that time—I was willing to go. But it was not to be. It took eight years before I had the opportunity to go overseas. During the time 'between' I was posted to four different bases, took many courses, and was selected to be part of Special Operations Forces (SOF).

Details Of Posting

Depending on where you are posted, and the type of trade you have, and what you witness, you carry some secrets that you have to keep from your family and friends.

I was James Bond without the suit, handgun, or sweet car, but I had some secrets. This empowered me. I was overly proud. Really, I was not James Bond, but 'Q' without his intellect.

Ultimately, the people in PRETC waiting for courses in communication were transferred to Kingston.

So I had chosen communications—I felt it would be a great career for me. But I was never told that the course for my trade/employment was only given in English. To access the course, I'd have to score a certain mark for reading, writing, and oral skills, on a test that is standard for anyone who works for the government to be considered bilingual. Ideally, I should have been sent to a course to learn how to speak, write, and read English, but unfortunately I wasn't able to get one… so, I bought books, watched movies, and hung out with English speaking people.

I was eventually trained as a communication research operator (291) and was advised that my security clearance would take another year or two, so decided to re-muster because I had the need and urge to work and serve, not wait.

In the process of re-mustering, I made three choices. The fastest one of the three, the one where I could be trained soonest, was 'Resource Management Support'. At that point, I was posted back to CFB-Borden to the logistics training school.

My first official posting, once in my trade, was Ottawa, at the headquarters of the Navy. I stayed there just under two years as the only army element in the Navy unit. One of the Navy commanders told me I needed a bigger challenge and advised me to apply for Canadian Special Operations Forces Command (CANSOFCOM). With the support of my chain of command, I applied and went through testing.

Six months later, in 2011, I was posted in Ottawa (to a confidential location). Though I worked within different squadrons, I remained in that unit.

Each Day I Leave My Naïve World

At the Ops squadron, at 0900, we would meet in a conference room. There were two large screens which linked us with assets overseas or to an active mission. Depending on the threat level, the Commander of the unit would attend. If the threat was medium, the officer in charge of the squadron would take the Commander's seat. Also present were the Sergeant Major of the squadron, the officer in charge of intelligence gathering, the Officer in Charge (OC) of Inside Canada routine and Outside Canada routine, and other needed members.

The OC would start the meeting by announcing the headlines. The intel would follow, informing us of what was going on in Canada, and about activities outside Canada related to threats. Non-commissioned officers from logistics, mapping, and training, would speak about related incidents. There was nothing casual about the meetings. We were presented with the constant, active threats that our country faced—that is, maintaining the safety of the population spoken about in earlier chapters. The military is always working.

Following a meeting, the day would continue with tasks related to communication, but some days never really ended because, in times of high-alert emergencies, none of the members could be further than ninety-minutes from the base.

At the end of each day I was a little less naïve.

In 2015, a kind-hearted supervisor gave up her own opportunity for deployment so that I could go on an overseas mission. I was given two months' notice—plenty of time for me, an eager guy who, though engaged to be married, wanted to serve. Of note: my fiancé organized our wedding on her own; this is the way of military life where spouses and loved ones handle many things alone.

I was excited for the unknown. Sure, I had some fears, but the adventure was driving me. We travelled by commercial air on a fifteen hour flight whose passenger manifest included fourteen infants. A nightmare. Fortunately, I had a nice pill to make me sleep part of the trip—a necessity because work began as soon as we landed.

Being deployed was a brand-new challenge. I had no clue what to expect. What I did learn, over time, is that if you don't have any expectations you are not sad about what comes up.

Erbil

Erbil is one of the oldest cities in the world; established six thousand years BCE. It is also called Hawler. At one time it was known as Arbela. It is the capital of the Kurdistan region in northern Iraq. Various cultures have inhabited the city, including Persian, Greek, Roman, Mongol, Ottoman, and Turk.

When I was deployed, the Kurds were the largest ethnic group living in the city which had between 1.5 and 2 million citizens.

I was surprised at the lack of security at the airport when we landed in Erbil—for such an important airport there was little to none. Some of the guys who'd already deployed were waiting for us and drove us to the camp which was on the on the airport land—we were part of multiple forces there. The security to get on the military camp was greater than at the airport. Our section consisted of a few trailers which were quarters for about fourteen people each. There was a trailer that held a bathroom and showers. Our gym was under a tent.

The beauty of Erbil was outside the camp. It is a city of extremes—decadently rich areas abound, as do profoundly poor sections. A dirt road can run into an even rougher one which is lined with 'houses' that evidence people living in abject poverty. In comparison, another road turns into a street of luxury cars and ornate buildings.

At the center of the city stands the Erbil Citadel, an ancient structure dating back four thousand years (2000 BCE). Its oval shape encloses over a million square feet. The centre of this city has been claimed to be the oldest site in the world that has been continuously inhabited.

Put simply: I was mesmerized, just like a child might be as they look into a kaleidoscope for the first time—fully present in the magic that appears before the eye and then flows its colours through to the heart and soul.

Taking in the cultural differences was overwhelming in a wonderful way. The perfume of history is contained in every dusty breath—and I inhaled it all. Erbil's sunbeams seared generations of tradition into my skin. My own presence, seemingly insignificant, was acknowledged by the environment itself—I truly felt a part of the place; that it accepted me as it had millions of others over the centuries. Witnessing the activities in the markets, registering the chants of united prayers, became music to my ears and played a symphony of tradition. The city took me in her arms and wrapped me in historic, cultural passion. Mesmerized seems an understatement.

When I got used to being on guard, I could align my alertness along with my appreciation for the rich culture, and that included the chaotic nature of driving and drivers, transactions between vendors and customers, and the calmness surrounding such frenzied behaviour.

Within the stress was a stunning contrast—no signals used when turning or changing lanes (there were no lanes). Miraculously one sees few accidents—it just seems to work. The road system and drivers reminded me of Montréal, where people push through traffic without any measure of defensive-driving or acknowledgment of the rules of the road. Somehow, total confusion on the roadways became clear through an accepted way of driving without indicating intentions, without speed limits, or regard for any lanes. The language of traffic was spoken in horns. If someone wanted to overtake another driver, they simply leaned on the horn and did what they wanted to do.

Initially, the oil fumes shocked me. The casual-ness of people dealing with their environment and danger was striking. One time, we were driving through a town and there was a fire—I looked for an accident, but there was none. No accident, no people, just crude oil leaking out of the ground, so someone just lit it up and let it burn.

I was struck by the cultural differences between a young country like Canada and this old civilization, evolving over thousands of years (even though there are new buildings and some modern influence). We are rule-followers and have modern laws—they are not litigious and move to the rhythm of what seems to be a more natural order.

Overseas becomes your home. Your flag ripples in the breezes of your mind alongside the one of the country you are in. About a month after arriving in Erbil, we celebrated Canada Day—a bar-b-que and a poker game—with each juicy mouthful of chicken, with each ante, raise, fold, and show, each of our group was transported to their hometown in a virtual 'leave'.

It was a privilege to serve in Iraq. The old city of Erbil is a collection of jewels and, despite being posted there at a time of unrest and terrorist presence, the city taught me that even in dark times, there can be intense beauty.

You Don't Know How It Is... Until You Are In It

Before I joined the military, I watched some movies. I recall a drill sergeant screaming at people, soldiers keeping the same position for hours without complaining, soldiers doing an obstacle course. I had read about multiple wars: I've always been intrigued by the tactics, and what the world wars brought to our society—the scientific discoveries made because of them; the advances in industry and technology; the horror of experimentation. I'd been fascinated by all the secrets that have been leaked, and energized by how much more there is to learn. I think I was very curious about humans being able to face tragedy for others. I was a bold, stubborn, and blunt teenager.

Rarely do people talk about the day to day reality of the military world. It is one thing to voice your opinion about something you see in a movie, it is an other to live that reality.

Now that I've been in the military, I understand that it is interesting to see, read, and hear about it, but it will never describe the reality.

There I was, that stubborn kid, completely transformed. Re-wired. When our sergeants screamed at us because one of us did something wrong, deep inside I knew that I would be better to shut my trap. Being screamed at was better than receiving a punishment for talking back. In the military, I learned to respect leadership, even at the times when I didn't agree—especially those times. Also, being screamed at, being sworn at, and treated like 'shit', taught me not to be affected by others, and not to be offended by small things.

There is a big difference between agreeing and respecting. I can have my own vision, and respect yours.

Everyone Is My Enemy... Am I Becoming Crazy?

At a young age I learned that we all have enemies. I was rejected and bullied by the same kid in elementary school. I changed school in the middle of elementary to attend a school that focussed on singing, and my first grade of high school I started at another. In that new school I found this same kid who hadn't forgotten about me, and who would bully me once more. He was my enemy; he was the one who raised others against me. I felt unappreciated and unwanted.

As I got older, the face of my enemies changed. When I joined the military there was a thought that we would go to war against the Taliban. Those were the ones we had to get rid of. Those were the ones who were attempting to steal our lives. The military made sure that we believed it.

One day, during my posting in Ottawa, we received an email stating that we should not travel in our military uniform, and we should not mention that we are serving our country. There was a new enemy, called ISIS (ISIL). They were hunting us in our own country. Not too long after, Corporal Nathan F. Cirillo was killed while on ceremonial sentry duty in Ottawa.

The killer was not Taliban. He was a lone wolf. The enemy was recruiting people who were looking to be part of something bigger; willing to sacrifice their life. The lone wolves could be (and were being) influenced by an organization—easily turned, simply radicalized. Those unstable individuals wanted to seek revenge, be recognized, or both. The world became even more dangerous, and ISIS took responsibility for many attacks. ISIS became the fear. They recruited people from Canada—'membership' was discreetly advertised, even directing, online, how to travel to their home base in Syria.

While deployed in Iraq, my enemy could be anywhere as soon as I left the base. I only felt safe on the base.

When I returned to Canada, and left the military, there was no 'back to base' safety. I kept a knife by my side. I sought a firearm license. My world was not so safe after all.

Time For Change

When I returned from deployment, I wanted to help my community more directly. I began the path of becoming a police officer.

The military is not like other employers. You belong to them. You have to. How else could a military mindset be built in order to protect the citizens of the country the military serves?

When a person signs with the military, depending on the job they take, they may sign a first contract of 3–7 years, and then a 25 year contract. In that, each person agrees that, if the time comes to leave before that, six month's notice must be given. After that, permission to leave will still be the decision of the military. I chose the 25 year contract.

This is how resignation works: first you have to write a memorandum to your Chain of Command reflecting the reasons for your request. At this first step, your CoC could deny your request. Remember, you belong to the Queen, you signed a contract.

The general timeline, from the day the memorandum is drafted, is six months. Obviously, over this period of wait, you attend work, with some meetings related to your release. It is a long process, but it has to be done.

I sent in my memo the day I was confirmed that I was accepted to attend police college in Calgary, Alberta.

OPERATION: WIRED DIFFERENTLY

BRIEFING EIGHT
OBJECTIVE: FROM CAMOUFLAGE TO A THIN BLUE LINE

September 2016. It seemed like one day I was a member of the Canadian Armed Forces, and the next I was in a panda car as a city police officer in Calgary, Alberta.

The decision to leave the military was made upon returning from Iraq. My soon-to-be wife and I wanted to have a child. The police force seemed the logical transition.

It was an adjustment to work 'on the street' rather than 'in the field'. I moved forward, getting used to married life, planning our family, then celebrating 'our' pregnancy and thinking about the future as a parent.

What I didn't do was address how adapting to civilian life was affecting my mental health. I did not realize how monumental the task was. Without realizing, I began to put my 'me' time aside—essentially, I did not attend to my mental health at all.

Of course, at the time, I didn't list these things daily as a litany of items weighing heavily on my mind—it was only in hindsight that I recognized how much I was dealing with (and therein lies the value of writing about one's life, officially or unofficially).

The day I became a police officer, I truly wanted to help my community. It became apparent, though, that 'everyone' was the enemy. Police officers are not typically appreciated in the majority of situations. People cannot own their faults. If I arrested someone for something, that person would blame me for their issues, stating I am arresting them because I am a white male—even when there was a warrant for their felony.

I am from Québec where the history between French and Indigenous is a close relationship due to having fought together against the English centuries ago. I had never been called a white man before. That shocked me.

The lack of accountability or unwillingness to accept responsibility is the same at 'lower level infractions': pull someone over for speeding and the police are the bad people because the driver is not at fault, the driver 'is late'.

I remember giving my first ticket for using a cellphone while driving. I was sweating, shaking, and stressed, although it was my job. The driver fought my ticket. Clearly she'd been using her phone while driving and put those around her at risk. She had broken the law. I was upset because it disturbed me that she couldn't own up to what she'd done wrong. The judge gave her a 'break' and she had to pay half the fine. It is like the system created to protect people has a 'barter, trade, discount, fifty-percent-off' counter. This is hugely inequitable to the public, and completely disheartening for the members of the force.

I continued in my career as an officer: I met other caring officers, I helped the general public, yet there was a difference. The culture was completely a grey one. Those grey areas were applicable to the civilian community we served and within the police department. It became difficult to trust parts of the organization in the same way I'd totally trusted the military, where every person took responsibility for their actions. And every person did take responsibility—they were forced to, there was no choice.

Was the grass greener in the military?

Police college involved a junior version of bootcamp. The police prioritize political correctness more than the military. The police force is about how people will see you—the military, while operating with strict codes of respect, is not quite as concerned about image; their actions and results convey the importance of their role. One is 'human' working with humans and the other is a 'soldier machine'.

In college I was tasered, pepper-sprayed, and had to fight with classmates. It was intense. But it was not like the military. On the street, working with other officers, the situations we were exposed to were dark, yet the connection between us did not come close to the brotherhood of the military, even though there is common ground between both forms of service: seeing people at their worst.

For the longest time, I wondered if the brotherhood in the military came to us because we were confined to a floor for five weeks and had to rely on each other. This is different than the police who go home after each shift to spend time with their family and friends who are not in the police force.

I do not recall one time in the police force when I was called to a nice, fantastic, outstanding situation. Why would I be? That's not the role of the police. People call the police to complain about something. Some officers would say it is the best show ever—sitting on the first row, seeing real life unfold. It is a career in which you have to wear dark humour to get through the surreal situations.

Sheepdog

Let's not be afraid of terms or expressions. The name sheepdog has been given to the police officer. It is not meant as a derogatory term. Simply put, the term refers to dedicated people (sheepdogs) who watch over the rest of the people (sheep).

Sheepdogs prevent the wolves (and other dangerous creatures or situations) from hurting the sheep. Sheepdogs understand that violence is sometimes necessary in order to protect the sheep. In most cases, the sheep do not like the sheepdog, preferring to go their merry way, oblivious to the perils of life.

At police college, a group of us wanted to create a 'patch' to represent our course. We decided, as a team, to have a sheepdog alongside the number of our course. We presented the idea to our chain of command and were immediately shut down. Apparently, if the population knew we felt this way—sheepdog and sheep—they would be upset to be seen as a herd of sheep. They would be against this 'term' because it sounded as if it was a putdown, but it is simply connected to a world they do not understand. My blunt military mentality went directly to this thought: the population were a bunch of sensitive people; so easily offended. Snowflakes. This was lesson one in the difference between the reality of military thinking and the passive (as I saw it: weak) attitude of the police organization which had even changed the term police force to police service because 'force' is too violent a word. On the sheep logo: I fought the decision of the officer higher in the chain of command, and lost.

Can we just be honest? Police officers confront the demons and evil of our society—the wolves. The sheep prefer not to. They choose not to see the dark side of truth; would rather remain naïve. And there is nothing wrong with being naïve in that sometimes it's better because some people cannot handle the truth.

There are a couple of ways people can remain naïve (not wanting to know the horrific things people do to each other): The first is 'not knowing' by choosing to close the door to all that is happening; the second is denial, a condition whereby the body, mind, and soul meet and decide 'there is no such thing as this horror, or that horror'.

The Games Sheep Play

I recall the sadness around the death of my uncle who was found in a brothel. Known to use cocaine and meth, he had overdosed. The police in Montréal had tagged him as a John Doe because he was found without ID.

My father phoned me—I was already a Calgary police officer at that time. He told me my mother had filed a missing person report, even though my father believed my uncle was likely dead. He asked me to act surprised when my mother informed me of the family's loss.

When she called, she said:

"Your uncle is gone…"

My answer was:

"Where did he go? Mexico? Hawaii?"

I knew I was lying, but I was also laughing… that was my coping mechanism protecting me, mixed with dark humour.

A few days later, my mother called. She cried and, seemingly unaware or unwilling to recognize the logical consequences of his choices, she went on to say that he'd been found at a hotel and that his heart had stopped. She continued with the story that she'd been in touch with the coroner and it was not an overdose, just a simple death. She said she knew this because the coroner had done a test and could not find any trace of drugs in his blood.

Having attended many overdoses as a police officer, I wondered what coroner would get involved with a John Doe. Clearly it was not just a 'hotel'. She argued that it was a simple death. I didn't agree. But I knew, in that moment, she wanted to 'keep' a good picture of her brother. In the face of all the facts, she needed to default to naïvety. I, however, am stoic.

Way back, when I heard my uncle's lifeless body was discovered in a hotel room, I knew why. I am, after all, a sheepdog. But others processed the situation differently. Some closed the door to what they knew. Others, like my mother, were in denial: "An overdose, in a brothel? No, he was my brother. Your uncle, he died of a heart attack."

Nevertheless, the deniers and the not wanting to know-ers remain in the same herd.

As a sheepdog, my blunt military training brings me into situations where people will be offended. In the military you cannot 'not' know things or deny them, but in civilian life you can. You can lock your door, not answer the phone, not speak to a relative; be as insular as your brain tells you to be. You can deny all you want, you can 'not want to know' to the end of the earth. And that is okay. But those people do not become first responders. And that is okay, too. More than okay. But it is hard for them to empathize with those same first responders. They are herded because they allow themselves to be, because they don't want to be the sheepdog and so, by default, they are the sheep. They want the protection. But they don't like that the canine nips at their heels.

The wolves in our society wear many costumes. The drugs, the thugs, the violence and all the dark aspects are those we know—some of our favourite television shows portray them. Why is it so hard to acknowledge that these elements are part of our lives? Is it terrifying to think such a thing could be up close and personal? Even within us?

I hold no anger toward my mother for believing the fantasy about her brother—I hold it out as an example: she is a highly educated, well traveled, experienced individual, yet she is one of many who can lie to themselves.

First responders, and the military, do what most of the sheep run away from. They choose that path for a number of reasons. They are wired differently, and they become further re-wired once in their chosen career.

NORMALIZING

I barely slept today. Night shift tonight. It is my last, then I have four days off. It is roughly 1630. I pack my lunch, kiss my wife and hug my son. I whisper in his ear that I am sorry that I have to go. He looks back at me with a smile. He doesn't understand, but I am sure he can feel my heart. I look at my wife, and can picture her as soon as I step outside; she will now wear the two hats for our son.

I climb into my vehicle and look up to the window—wave goodbye to them. She smiles back at me and I can feel her strength. I am amazed by her and thankful for her. I fire up the vehicle, set up my tunes to something angry and violent. I need to be ready for a good workout. On my way to my district, I drink my pre-workout shake so that when I get there I'll be pumped for a good session that will release some anxiety and stress. I drop my bag at my locker, grab my water, and lift some plates.

A hot shower follows the workout, with a quick shave and a swipe of product in my hair. I jump into the uniform. Lastly, I load my Glock and secure it in my holster. A magazine of 17 rounds, and one in the chamber. I make my way to the area where I ask for an SUV, a shotgun, taser, radio, and heavy armor. The heavy armor is the same we had in the military. As for the soft armour—the one officers wear under their shirt every shift—it is not that soft, and it won't even protect me from the caliber of firearm with which officers are supplied. I purchase my own soft armour of higher quality.

I do the routine of inspection of my patrol SUV (lights, sirens, camera), check for anything suspicious in or on the vehicle, load my shotgun and secure it. Next I log into my CAD (laptop). It is pretty robotic and relaxed. My radio is turned on, and I can listen if there is anything going berserk in the street. Now that my vehicle and I are ready to go, I can officially start and attend parade.

1855 hours. My breakfast (dinner) is warmed up. I'm waiting for the parade. My sergeant enters. We are not friends, but co-workers; we share small talk about my dinner. The line members show up in the next few minutes. To reflect on the term line member, it had been changed from team member because it was not reflecting what the group was. It was understood that we are not a team, but people who work on the same shift.

We are given documents that have been mailed or couriered—subpoenas, tickets to correct, paystubs. We are informed of the hotspots in our district, informed who we should watch for, and given any intel that has been received. Often, most of us would have too low of a security clearance to hear anything major.

Today, the sergeant shares that a drug dealer has been killed—shot a number of times. Now, in this situation, one would think there might be a certain sadness, but my train of thought reverts to military and an enemy mindset. I can hear the voice in my head right now: "Play stupid games, win stupid prize."

I realize this sounds harsh, heartless, cold. But it is the way the military must think in order to protect the citizens of the country they serve. If that collective mentality, through training, through rewiring, had not been present, one second, less than one second, could see others harmed, killed, a community massacred.

As I am being briefed, I smile. One asshole less to deal with.

The shooter has not been found. Forensics has not had time to examine the scene, so continuity of scene is necessary. No police officer likes to do that type of duty. All it means is sitting at a grizzly scene waiting for someone or for forensics to take over. I am not an awesome person but, because I am the youngest officer in the group, I volunteer for the continuity. I'll serve my time.

I make my way to the residence after grabbing an extra-large coffee. I will need to be in this house for twelve hours. I bring my lunch, cellphone charger, and that coffee.

I can tell it is a drug house. It's dirty. There's a distinct smell of total negligence. This is not a home. Death hangs in the air, too. There is a large bloodstain on the floor and I can see that he must have crawled a bit after he was shot. There are seven shell cases—9mm, pretty standard. The wall tells a story, and I know where he was standing prior to being shot because of the 'blood art' on the beige. The shooter must have been stressed, his finger not solid on the trigger, hence missing his target and creating holes in the wall.

I sign on to this duty and the previous officer signs off. He tells me the bathrooms are too disgusting to use—that the whole place is a shithole. He looks at my extra-large coffee and tells me I am brighter than he is. I highly doubt I'll drink all the coffee, but it will be my toilet.

I sit at the murder scene. I text my wife for a while to cope with where I am. It is dinner time… well, it is roughly midnight. I stand in the middle of the scene, making sure not to step where I shouldn't, and I take a bite of my sandwich.

Up close I can blink, and the nano second my eyes are closed I can pretend the bread is freshly baked and I'm somewhere else. The flavour is delicious. I savour the tuna, and appreciate how I've added just the right amount of mayo. I chomp away, a working guy on the job.

It is not that I don't have a heart… or that I don't feel. The only way I can cope with all of it is to go on with my life. In the presence of such a vile situation of life gone bad for someone else, I must do normal things. That means eating. I smile. The tuna sandwich is amazing and I am happy to be alive and not be the guy whose blood is spattered all around me.

At 0630 hours, another officer arrives. We are still continuing to secure the scene. He asks me for my thoughts. I give him my observations. I return to the office, do everything I did at the beginning of my shift, but in reverse order. I drive home way above the speed limit. No music. I want to be home. To real. To normal. Not my normal, I want my family's normal—the naïve view, their carefree attitude.

I hug my son—the life in him greets me like the biggest sunshine ever. I kiss my wife on her lips. She asks me about my night. I tell her it was pretty quiet—nothing unusual. She smiles that smile that she knows I am not telling the truth because I don't want her to know. It's better that way. Safer. Why should she have to feel like I do? I look at both of them, and tell them that I will be back—that is my code to say I am going to bed. I miss both of them, as I slide between the sheets.

Death Visits Weekly

I remember the first suicide I attended as a police officer—day seven of being a cop: parts of his feet were yellow, other parts were black. We had to unhook him from his rope. I don't think anyone is ever prepared for that type of scene. The visuals, the smell, the tension—it stays with you; it sticks to you.

At another call, it is the sound that features heavily: sadness, amplified as screams from a mother of a child who has passed, pierces your heart.

When we are not walking with death, we are sitting with it, but never able to run away from it. It is our commitment as first responders.

There's the girl that didn't succeed. And the momentary danger that followed because she survived. Sadly, a young student had expressed to her family that she was lonely and didn't know what to do, therefore she was thinking of ending her life.

Not an unusual call, really. There are a lot of lonely people, and so many of them consider a way out, and call for help. They shout to family, to friends, but often it is the police who attend. Someone always answers 9-1-1.

At such a call, officers check for weapons that can be used against them, or could hurt the person who is attempting to take their life. We check for medication, and evaluate the state of mind to work out how to communicate with the person. All of that in a short time—minutes.

It is clear in my mind:

She was in her bed. She had a butcher knife at her throat—pretty common to find that pairing: knife and dark thoughts. We were able to remove the knife. I was up close. We discovered seven more knives under the heavy duvet. We hadn't thought about that. Seven knives, any of which could have been used against her, or us. There is always a first time.

She survived. Sweet girl. No one deserves to be in such a dark place. She lives on, as far as I know, in real life.

But in my nightmares, she does not. She goes the whole way. Night after night, I witness it all, and smell her blood as she slices the butcher knife across and through her throat.

Is Life Fair? No.

I need to adapt to the 'no' because it is the world in which my son will be raised. I will have to explain to him, in time, what the reality is. But, for now, I believe that he has to remain naïve. He is learning to look both ways before he crosses the road, but he doesn't know that I attended the death of a civilian who crossed the street and was struck by an impaired driver. Or that, sadly, the driver was never charged because no witnesses want to testify, or worse: the crown prosecutor does not want to go forward with charges.

My two employers confirmed for me that life is not fair. It may be wondrous, a miracle, an ecstatic experience between an orange sunrise and a purple sunset, but it is not fair.

Even More Unfair

What if you are a horrible soldier or horrible police officer? What happens to you?

Have you ever heard of a "promoted & posted"? It is very simple: if you are not liked and it seems like they cannot get rid of you, you are promoted and then posted. In this case, your rank changes, and you find yourself in a terrible location because you are a shit pump. It is hard to be fired in either world. In the military you've signed a contract; they can keep you and make you miserable on your way out. In the police, there is no contract, so the exit is a usually a shorter process. However, the police have been known to give the problem to another unit, assign them to a special 'position' and leave them to rot.

There is a police association that will protect you from this—for the most part. The sad part is, if you are a shitty cop, you should be punished—there is nothing a cop hates more than a 'bad cop'. But the association runs interference. Too much.

Reality Versus Television

Movies and television shows are not realistic. It took me hours to do my first warrant. How is it possible in the movies it takes minutes? A report for drinking and driving took hours. The irony? I released the offender and had to work five more hours (after his release) to complete the report.

Criminals do not stay in jail until they die—I wish they would; they sometimes get released before the officer is finished the paperwork. It is not true that the system is on the side of the law; it is on the side of the money. Who has the deepest pockets? I developed a hatred about how the system works. Even if I know the offender's identity and have evidence, if that evidence is not what the crown prosecutor is looking for, then I'd better not charge the offender—the charge will be dropped before it goes to court.

When Do People Become Victims?

When they feel violated? Is it that they are victims or just not accepting what is going on? Why is it necessary to involve first responders when the situation is not a 'life or death' event or not even a crime?

Taxpayers pay for the police to serve and protect, not to parent adults.

There are some days when adults are not adults. At those times they contact first responders.

At times, I have seriously thought someone should slap the reasoning back into the head of some callers. There are calls over which I've had to shake my head. Over time, I believe I became jaded and stopped having faith in society. There were times when I wanted to escape to an island—to not give a shit about the world.

An actual call I attended: a husband, so upset that his wife put too much salt in his dinner, he called the police.

Yes, I understand this is a mental health issue, but again… a first responder to the scene? We have to attend; we have an obligation to attend all calls.

The parenting scenario is a common one. I recall attending a mother who was not able to handle her four year old—he wouldn't go to bed—so she called us to put him to bed.

This one was interesting—why can't we grow up? A frustrated guy calls us because he was not invited to his neighbour's wedding. To create grief for them he complains about the noise. These are sounds of celebration, and love. Unreal.

An unusual one was this: The train is no longer running as it is too late at night. A female calls the police alleging she has been robbed. We reviewed the cameras; she was alone the whole time at the train station—

the whole time until she left with us. Nothing had happened to her. She just wanted a ride home.

One I'll never forget is the missing cat. The owner swore that the cat had been kidnapped. I discover it is an outdoor cat. It is missing. No one kidnapped it. But her insistence was over-the-top. She was convinced.

The cat kidnapping was another waste of time… and yet it was a cry from someone who needed to have connection. Clearly mental health issues.

Another call, common to many officers: members of the public's total lack of being able to mediate a situation. A homeowner wants his renter out, therefore he calls the police three times a day to make the renter's life a living hell—no concern that those 36 calls, and subsequent attending the renter's residence, could be taking time away from a real emergency. It is a crime to abuse the system or call 911 without having an emergency, but the service would never approve to charge anyone, because it will make the population doubt the ability of first responders to respond.

I'll close with the lady who found a grass snake. Yes, she called 9-1-1.

There are dozens more examples—some that would make you fall off your chair.

The thing is, it's the sadness of it all. If you read them again, take a look at how much sadness is behind the reasons for the call; how maladjusted the adult involved is. Then there are the economics: the wasted time of paid officers. I didn't become a police officer to drive someone home who could have called a taxi. I, like other officers, joined the force to help true victims, to make the community safe, to make sure all families can sleep peacefully.

So what is a true victim? I asked a few of my colleagues without telling them they would end up in a book. (Surprise, if you are reading it now.)

- Someone that suffers from an Incident that is a direct result of someone else's action, whether physical or mental.
- A victim is someone who has lost something or had someone else's will imposed on them.
- A true victim is anyone who has been harmed mentally / physically / emotionally by another person.
- A victim of crime: someone who has had a criminal offence committed against them.

As you can see, those answers are pretty much the same, just worded differently.

Now, let's look what the dictionary tells us:

victim
vik-tim

noun
a person who suffers from a destructive or injurious action or agency: *a victim of an automobile accident.*

a person who is deceived or cheated, as by his or her own emotions or ignorance, by the dishonesty of others, or by some impersonal agency: *a victim of misplaced confidence; the victim of a swindler; a victim of an optical illusion.*

a person or animal sacrificed or regarded as sacrificed: *war victims.*

a living creature sacrificed in religious rites.

From https://www.dictionary.com/browse/victim

I believe all those 'definitions' are true and real. I am on board with my colleagues and the dictionary. If we remove the factor of compassion and empathy, this is my perspective on it: a victim is **NOT** someone who *feels* victimized… and… we can all feel victimized for many reasons, because we were not understood, respected, heard, or were upset another party does not agree with us.

But… coming across someone who had been robbed, assaulted, taken advantage of by fraud, was (and is) a true victim to me. It is not someone who tries to gain from the system for their own purpose.

Having been exposed to so many situations, I found that some were less important than others. I questioned whether I'd lost my compassion—and still do. I believed that the 'true victim' filled me with energy to make me stronger for the next calls. And for the calls I considered 'less important—not victims', I found they drained me. In the end, many callers needed help—and will continue to—but they are not victims of a crime.

Over time, I became anxious. I didn't know if it was the past military, or the current policing experiences, or a combination of both. When I began to see all the areas of grey (people getting away with things, no firm rules, and the exhaustion that causes for officers) the anxiety built. I still did my job to the fullest; that impulse to run into a burning building rather than away from it was still there. Perhaps even more.

I used humour to diffuse so many situations. Being French Canadian, I would come into a highly tense situation, perhaps one with a high probability of physical interaction, or a severe domestic violence scene, and raise my arms and say, "It's okay, the French police is here." I was the Robin Williams of policing. The Chris Rock of law enforcement. I brought the dark humour of Bon Cop Bad Cop into the room, and magically lit up a scene so that even a hardened criminal would crack a smile as the crazy French cop made himself the 'negative'—poked fun at himself. It worked well. I know I saved situations from becoming more serious. But it took its toll.

At home, I had a security system installed—cameras and sensors. I'd lock my doors in the middle of the day. I became concerned with being able to protect my wife and son. I knew too much about the world—from the military. I knew too much about the city—from the police. And, in my small town, a bedroom community close to the city where I policed, I felt the evil closing in. I was vigilant about protecting my wife and son. The thing is, I had been in a car chase that went past my home… the darkness could drive to my town. I knew my neighbour was a supporter of the Hells Angels. I knew that a block away from my house lived a gang member. I didn't police in my community, on purpose. Many officers do not police where they live. We don't want to know there is a criminal element—on purpose ignore it to get some sense of a normal life.

When I hit the wall for the second time—metaphorically, of course—nothing was safe. I kept track of which vehicles drove down my alley, and who came to the door. I could not trust the world. I stopped contacting police officers that I had developed friendships with. I feared my neighbours—they could be against me.

It was as if I was wearing sunglasses but, instead of blocking the sun, it was blocking all the good things in the world—everything was filtered by a visceral darkness.

Food for thought…

Let me ask you something: do you see some thief who gets his property stolen a victim? Or is it karma?

Someone who rapes multiple victims, then, while incarcerated, is raped multiple times. Is he a victim or is it karma? I say he deserves the full extent of it.

OPERATION: WIRED DIFFERENTLY

BRIEFING NINE
OBJECTIVE: COMPASSION FATIGUE

Compassion fatigue is also called vicarious traumatization. Those who help people or animals in distress can also find themselves in distress—secondary to the 'client' (that animal or person they are helping). Over time, it manifests as reduced compassion for those they are helping. It is common for those who work directly with 'victims' to be affected.

The symptoms include a shift in the view of the world, and a kind of cynicism toward life and life situations. Quick to become irritable, their experiences of pleasure are decreased from what they used to be. Physical exhaustion is often present. Situational depression lasts longer, and eventually becomes a kind of permanent depression. Impaired judgement, based on an overarching negative perspective, is common. Compassion fatigue impacts both professional and personal life.

First recognized among healthcare workers, further studies confirmed other professions were at risk—this included law enforcement personnel, including dispatchers who are constantly receiving calls from people who are facing emergencies, then having to take action to keep them calm while assessing how to rate and then assign the issue. With dispatchers, their input is a kind of 'isolated' type because they are not on scene and don't see the outcome of the situation—therefore not able to bring closure.

The key to preventing compassion fatigue is openness in speaking about it. Organizations that support empathetic views and welcome discussion are likely to have fewer cases of compassion fatigue—and therefore PTSD—than those who have the 'suck it up' attitude, or 'it's part of the job' mindset.

When my son needed me…
When My wife was crying,
Even if I was sitting on a chair across from her,
She couldn't reach me.
My eyes were staring into the abyss of dissociation.

I walked those hallways,
Despite everyone seeing me,
The ghost of every trauma I carry,
Took over my life.
I am wounded, because I stopped caring about me.

Demons do not only come at night,
Nightmares come during the day as well,
They came to my life, and never left,
In the darkness of the sun.
I walk with them and learn how to live,
Carrying them on me.

Accountability

The police are investigated for everything and, when they're not, they're criticized and, when they're not, they're not trusted.

The man hit a van full of kids. He is drunk. He calls his wife.

Five hours of paperwork later…

The charges are dropped. He did not call a lawyer. No one saw him hit that vehicle. While the police wanted the charge, the crown prosecutor says it will be tough to charge. They only want to win.

Two kids call 9-1-1 by mistake. I have to check. It is a nice house, in an upscale neighbourhood. I finally make contact with the occupants of the house. A fifteen year old kid. He is afraid. He tells me, 'You are threatening.'

I explain that I am not.

He says, 'You have a gun.'

But my gun is still in my holster. The gun never left my holster, nor was my hand ever on my firearm.

I am in shock. He's never had a bad encounter. Seemingly, he's in a nice home. He's been raised to hate me.

From his parents?
Social media influence?
The television show, Cops?
Why has he been raised to hate the police?

Another strange call. From a child. Allegedly, he's been robbed. I attend the call. His mother has taken his Tablet away. The child can't handle it.

The mom can't handle it. 'It' being life. She has seven children. Her husband is in jail. The child has not been robbed, he has been punished for not attending school, but since he called the police, the police have to attend and ascertain where the Tablet is, and why it was taken.

In this case, parenting is required, not policing. Where do we draw the line?

Rarely is there closure for an officer with the people they deal with. Mainly there is chaos, and unsettled people. I never see an outcome… this person changed their ways… another person found their true path… an individual reported back and thanked for the intervention… too many situations are unresolved. I struggle to find the meaning when there is no closure. I'm not asking for a happily ever after, I'm asking for just an after.

Nothing is minor. No matter how small things seem, every call seems tragic to the caller, whether the outcome is that a kid doesn't have his Tablet or someone is murdered—the dysfunction is everywhere.

A troubled kid, already in a group home, has broken everything in his room. We have a warrant to take him to the hospital because he hadn't taken his meds. It's not my first visit with him—but he doesn't recognize me. Why would he remember me? People don't remember us personally, they see the uniform. Nevertheless, I connect with him and he calms. He's a large teenager—about 350 pounds. It was easy for him to snap chairs and crush a table.

I later discover that in the past week it took four police officers to take him down.

The following week he is in the news; he has killed his caregiver in the group home. The system is not working for the victim because there is no punishment. The system is not working for the kid—who were his parents, and their parents? He's a mess and there is no end to his rage.

In the police system, there is no time for closure, and the department is not designed for it. We have to make peace with what happens. But it is hard to make peace. I am so busy working, and I want closure: I want black and white (not grey) rules and, among it all, I begin to forget how to feel.

My dreams begin to include scent. While I sleep, I smell my own fear. Fuck, this perfume reeks of my previous call.

The cry of a child pierces my deepest sleep. I am on a call… it is a kidnapping. A child. "Daddy, Daddy, where are you?" A random voice. No… it is my son. He is sobbing unceasingly. He has lost me. I am gone.

I wake in a sweat. Another nightmare. I now have a museum of recurring dreams—terrifying ones. Various calls distort into even more horrifying productions. Suicidal student, she kills herself most nights. My son, his crying is relentless and heartbreaking. I curate the scenes in my sleep as if walking through a gallery—but these dreams are not works of art. My bed is not a safe place anymore. I turn to napping—there is some protection in the short sleep.

A few colleagues ask if I am okay. I maintain my humour… no, I darken it. I am joking… "French police on the scene. The silly French man is here." "Crazy French cop, everybody freeze." I must save the people. All the people. All of them but me.

I am reminded that I must secure
a scene before try to save someone.
Your own oxygen mask, Jon.
But I do not listen.
I am the water swirling down the drain.
The child's spinning top turning and turning.
I am the threads of my DNA—a fraying helix.
The downward spiral.
Please.
Catch me.

The war within…
Morning, my friend, you woke me up early,
How did you sleep?
You kept me up,
You made me toss and turn and sweat,
You even visited me in my dream world.

Your visit was not needed,
I could have done without it,
You tell me you are protecting me,
By hiding the past,
In a space in my brain that I am not aware of.

All of a sudden you are bringing it back,
When I could have done without.

Now if I ignore you,
You talk to my muscles,
And make them twitch,
Talk to my subconscious,
And invade my dreams,
As if they were yours.

You make me fear the world.
When years ago, I would not have been stopped by anything,
You create a paranoia,
To the point that my blinds are closed,
So I can't see what the world is up to.

You create a war inside of me,
The fearful boy wants to run,
While the soldier wants to face you,
Those two can't agree on what to do.

Calm, I am sitting at the table with my family,
While inside I am screaming as loud as I can't scream outwardly,
I am looking at my wife, my eyes empty,
The words can't come out… please take me in your arms.

They say keep your friend close and your enemy closer,
Allow me to lie, and call you my friend ,
Come close to me ,
Because I have got enough of letting you direct my life.

I fought the enemy before,
I am done being your target,
I am ready for this war,
This war within,
Because we have never been friend.

A rage, that boiled in my veins…
I think that deeply I knew about it,
I ignored it, I didn't want to be seen as weak,
I couldn't face the judgement,
Because as much as people say, it is okay.
They speak when you are gone.
Like a knife, words are stabbing my soul.

It was easier to wear a mask,
And push out more energy,
So nobody realized that I am not okay.

It is human to compare,
I can hear them saying that I didn't see anything,
That I didn't go through anything dramatic,
Some have been through worse,
And probably some did,
But this is my hell.

I am the one who has to fight it,
Not you, nor them.

This "them" were the brothers and sisters,
The ones who maybe don't want to see,
That they are broken too.
That they fear what I go through,
Because they have those nightmares.

The ones that make them wake up with cold sweat down their spine,
Where you are in panic, and can't fight,
Just want to flight,
Because they already lost the battle.

By ignoring the signs that life gave me,
I dug a hole, far deeper than six feet,
Just so I am not seen as weak,
I still hold this shovel.

For the ones who whisper at my back,
That I shouldn't complain,
That I was not in a gun fight,
That I have never been in the explosion of an IED.
I still have all my limbs,
I was just communications or logistics,
The little guy who stayed behind the lines.

I was told that you get used to seeing dead bodies,
The first one is the one that remains in your brain,
Why do I remember all their faces?
Eyes closed or not.
They still live in my dreams,
The dreams you have when you are still awake.

The cries from the family members,
The screams my heart made in silence,
Because I could not show that I had feelings,
I had to be professional and that is the double standard,
It is expected to see horrors in this profession,
But it is not expected to be hurt.

I wear a uniform and my humanity is gone,
That's what the population thinks or is it what they want,
But I am a husband, a father, a son,
Like them I hope for the day peace will join the sunrise,
And never go to bed.

I don't mind if I don't have a job anymore,
I am not in it for the money,
I do it for them, who see me as the bad guy,
For them who are so quick to judge me,
And tarnish my name, that name they can't even say,
But rather call me by insults.

Trust me, I am my own worst enemy,
I can judge myself, and I do it over and over again,
I don't need anyone to do that.

I have rage from the moment I wake up,
To when I go to sleep,
I wonder why me? Why, God? Why?
I did what you asked me,
I fulfilled my orders,
I did this job, that nobody wants to do,
I sacrificed so much.

I am no angel, but I did what life requested from me,
I missed my wife's birthday,
I left her many nights to sleep alone,
My son will never know that the day he was born,
I was answering a domestic violence complaint.

I thought I was tougher, I thought I had all the tools to cope,
That my shield would protect me,
That I would never bring pain at home,
That work would stay at work,
Like a haunting, the ghost followed me,
Followed me home.

Slowly in my life,
It started to move some pieces of the puzzle in my heart.
Some of those pieces should have never been moved there,
When the damage was done,
The ghost was now comfortable.

Since I am seen as someone who is contagious,
The ones that I called co-workers, brothers and sisters,
Don't call me anymore,
Guilty by association, maybe they will be ill.
I find myself alone,
Yet I am told it is a fight that I can't fight on my own.

OPERATION: WIRED DIFFERENTLY

BRIEFING TEN
OBJECTIVE: THE FIRST WALL

On December 30, 2017, the world stopped for a moment and became a more wondrous place for me. Our child was born. I became a parent. A father. I now had a son. Nothing would ever be the same. The house would soften its edges and change its contents, there would be a car seat seemingly forever in my peripheral, blankets would smell of baby, strollers a way of life, a highchair marking the position of where sooner than I could recite a nursery rhyme, a little boy would sit and tell me he was all grown up and leaving home.

I. Became. A. Parent.

About six weeks after our son's birth, we headed to Florida, to spend some much needed down-time in my in-laws' condo, with my in-laws and our son. My wife had not had an easy pregnancy. Her body deserved sun, her mind needed the ocean's song, and the support of her parents would allow us to spend time together and as a family since I had not had a break in over two years.

I never knew that the break would be literal—the first visible crack in me.

The ocean was every colour of blue a travel brochure promises. Each tucked into a kayak, we paddled on a magical surface, one with the waves. The salt on my lips and the breeze bringing the sun's rays to my face and my arms was a balm to my aching self. In an absorbed peace, I allowed the oars to rest and, as if choreographed, glistening silver creatures broke through the water's surface, leaping in their dolphin ways, touching my soul, engaging my reverence of nature. I was alive with a surge of loving lifeforce. My son was back in the condo, safe in the arms of his grandparents. I was a father. This. This. This… was peace. I could breathe. So many years of not breathing. No breaks. I bathed in the love of the planet—diamonds on the tips of the waves moving my kayak. My eyes teared. Joy, ease, contentment and… then… in a heartbeat… it was all gone.

Gone. The tears were sorrowful and flowed in a tempestuous storm. I was in the eye of my own hurricane, being pushed to the edges into spinning winds that began to rip apart my life-so-far. Darkness flooded my vision. All the diamonds gone. The dolphins deep below the surface. Organ by organ shut down to the bare minimum for survival. The kayak drifted toward a lagoon-like place filled with a tangle of weeds.

I was no longer a husband, father, son, brother. I was nothing.

As the kayak touched the weeds, my wife appeared beside me in her craft. There was fear in her eyes. Her lips were moving. She was asking me what was wrong? What happened?

"I can't do it."

"It's too hard."

"I said it's too hard. "

"I can't do it. I can't move."

Somehow—her emotional and physical strength is more powerful than any superhero—she managed me and her and our boats to the shore.

The next thing I was in our room in the condo. Just me, my cellphone, and an episode of panic that chased fear to a new level. "Keep this quiet," an inner voice said to me. "If you share it with your current employer, you might lose your job."

Terrified, I moved through an hour or ten, then frantically searched for a number for my previous carers… the military… Veterans Affairs. "Remember, no one else needs to know," said that voice. "You'll be seen as weak, you fucking loser."

I called anyway. They set me up to meet with someone on my return.

I returned from Florida two days before my wife and son—scheduled to work. I got on the plane—a zombie at 35,000 feet—and not long after landing, I clocked in, checked my vehicle, signed out my gun, attended the briefing, and put on the bullet proof vest that protected me from the weapons of bad guys and prevented my own feelings from coming past the surface of my chest and…

just like the crises of others I'd attended—the suicides, the car accidents, stabbings, rapes, and associated perceived pathetic cries for help that were really humans reaching out for contact—I pushed my own trauma under the car mats, toed them under the area rug in front of the sofa, put them in a box and shoved them under the bed.

Swallowing the words of counselling in the equivalent of taking a baby aspirin for a migraine, I attended six sessions with a representative from Veterans Affairs, using their advice as a broom to keep sweeping my heart under the carpet. On the job, I 'd say I'm fine. It echoes back to me. You are weak if you say anything else.

"Crazy Frenchman on scene," I'd continue to say at calls where I could diffuse tense situations and get a perpetrator or victim to calm, submit, smile, forget the moment. But inside, the comic, the creative, the problem solver had left the building.

I went through the rest of the year holding hands with the inevitable crash and burn, squeezing it so tight that I could block its breath and kill it. I squeezed and squeezed and waited for something to click into place and tell me it was okay. "*This is normal and just a phase, you're okay now. Everyone goes through this. It's all gone. There, there, Jon. All better, now.*" But no amount of torque could choke it.

THE COW JUMPED OVER THE MOON

It doesn't matter if you believe in legends, superstition, or spells, the shifts at full moon are intense. Ask any teacher if the mood of their students changes when there is a full moon. Every ER nurse and doctor will share there's a surge in emergencies at that time of the month—and bizarre injuries as well. Even in the calm of my home, my son wakes more when the moon is full.

On the job, in the police force, a full moon means a full shift.

I asked a few friends from my community of first responders to share what is the first thing that comes to mind when they had to do a night shift on a full moon. Here are the answers.

"Gonna be a lot of crazy bitches out tonight." Julie

"Nooooooooooo." Laura

"Here we go baby!" Travis.

"Oh, Fuck." Gore

"I hope I don't see a black cat." Teresa

"Here it comes." Dave.

Don't get me wrong, I love helping, but sometimes those nights would be overwhelming. It seemed like the number of calls doubled. Incidentally, this was the night of the student with the hunting knife to her throat… the girl who had seven additional knives in her bed, which we found after I'd calmed her and carefully removed the one she had at her throat.

Overdoses are pretty common, but finding a naked man in the middle of the road in excited delirium in the middle of the winter is not totally normal—but on a full moon? Of course. He should be frozen. But perhaps his body is kept alive by some planetary power.

HAVING A CHILD IN THIS WORLD

I am a family man now, father of a little one, and husband to a woman who challenges me every day. We have three puppies. We are the quintessential family. After seeing the true human side, the horrible traits that we carry, the horrors that are done daily… I wonder if I am selfish to bring a child into this world. I do not doubt the love that I have for him. But the world seen from my eyes is not something that is nice and fluffy.

la vie n'est pas rose

Before this world gets better, it will become worse. It is like a clock's pendulum swinging from one extreme to another. Like I wrote in one of my poems, a piece which inspired me to write this book, I see the darkness of our world before I see the brightness of it. It is probably a way to protect me. Maybe it is from my training, but just as I would not venture into a war zone without having gathered intelligence, I behave the same way with daily living.

We are in Canada, a beautiful country. We have terrorist sleeper cells implanted in various big cities, the mafia, the biker gangs, the extremists, and many others. This is the reality I live in. Before my wife gave birth, I asked myself if I would share this knowledge with my son. I came to the answer that I would not. I do not want my son to live in fear, or sense potential danger every time he goes out.

I decided that I will give him the tools to confront challenges that life will bring to him.

My father told me about me being his legacy, and I want my son to be mine.

I believe, as parents, we have a responsibility toward our children. I will show my son the path as his guide, but I do not foresee holding his hand through life.

In talking to my friend who is a correctional officer (jail guard), she told me that she does not want to have a child. She says she has no desire to bring a kid into a world like ours. I understand her. Can you believe working forty-eight hours a week with the one percent of the population who constantly break the law; living in a world where you are constantly on your guard, where you can not trust anyone? I would see the world way darker than I can see it now.

Corrections officers are the often forgotten sheepdogs that make sure the wolves don't run freely. I am so thankful for their sacrifice.

In the police force, it is a totally different ball game. Officers still protect the sheep, but are not always completely surrounded by predators; they have a variety of people and situations to deal with.

THEATRE OF THE MIND
A POWER PLAY BY JON A. ARCHAMBAULT

Lobby
Check your coat
Usher
Program
Find your seat
House lights dimmed
Inhale

THE MEETING (A TRAGEDY)
A ONE ACT PLAY BY JON ARCHAMBAULT-AYOTTE

SYNOPSIS: A young man speaks to the various layers of himself, and encounters previously unseen enemies with whom he must interact, and accept their presence.

SETTING: A generic, one-doored room containing a table and chairs in any house, Anytown, Canada.

CHARACTERS:

SELF Aka JON ARCHAMBAULT-AYOTTE is aka HIGHER SELF on an exceptional day – of which there aren't many lately. Exhausted, in robot mode, this former military now police officer, always ready to serve, is worse for wear, fighting for control of his mind, looking for any way to get out of the line of fire, trying best not to crumble under pressure. He calls a meeting to call his attributes to action in an 'it's time to work together to save ourself.'

SUBCONSCIOUS SELF's conjoined twin. Mostly aligned with its sibling, has a capacity for deeper thought than SELF and can shapeshift to fully encompass the essence of JON.

BRAIN By the book… what grey area? A hard-ass in army boots with high expectations and a penchant for rules and roles, BRAIN would dive in again if called to be a first quick responder. But lately, BRAIN's decision making has been affected by an intruder.

HEART An electrical and magnetic character having trouble with crossed signals. Typically empathetic, a lifetime poet and romantic, HEART is sick of dealing with frayed wires, and tired of coming second, scared to lead because of the pain it witnesses through emotion, inside and outside, daily.

SOUL HEART's mentor, precariously perched atop a communications tower, desperately attempting to fix the faulty system that connects all members to a higher power.

BODY Fatigued from dodging and blocking punches, weary from repairing tears on its uniform, body barely has the strength to push 'the connect to team' button – though BODY doubts it would work anyway.

SURPRISE CHARACTERS:

PTSD An expert in covert operations; a master of disguise, dark and untrustworthy – some say a double agent—PTSD lurks rather than marches.

DEPRESSION PTSD's sidekick. Follows orders. Will do anything for PTSD's approval. Never seems to be able please PTSD with his efforts. Nevertheless, DEPRESSION likes expectations, loves to disappoint. Thrives on lethargy. Is 'all in' with alcohol fueled sessions; stomps loudly the morning after. Favourite colour: muddy brown-grey

DISSOCIATION A specialist in illusion, a magician in a former life. Loves a blackout. Famous words: "Now it's here, now it's not… fooled you, it's still there, just behind this false screen."

FADE IN

ACT I

SCENE 1

Stage direction: three dark characters in background. HEART and SOUL sitting at table—each with a coffee mug. BRAIN, SUBCONSCIOUS, and BODY nearby, standing facing each other, appear to be chatting quietly. SELF is observing them all from a distance away, closer to audience.

SELF: It's time for a meeting. Should I gather everyone like when I was serving? By rank, everyone at attention? Maybe I should be more relaxed, have a round table where everyone can express equally. Some of the members of this team are louder than the others; I'll need to hold a place for each one of them to make sure none are bullied.

Stage direction: SELF moves toward the two groups. The dark characters are seemingly unnoticed at the back of the room.

SELF: Form up in two ranks. Attention! Answer your name when you are called. BRAIN. HEART. SOUL. BODY. I see there are others here. Excuse me, this is a closed meeting.

Stage direction: the three dark characters move toward the door, open it, and leave, but as soon as SELF's back is turned on them and to the table area, they re-enter and casually lean against the doorframe and wall beside it.

Muttered versions of 'present' are audible, yet a committed and solid physical response takes place from HEART, SOUL, BRAIN, SUBCONSCIOUS (who wasn't called) and BODY. It goes like this: slide the right foot to centre, lift the left leg by raising knee, plant the left foot beside the right foot, stick out chest—proud like you mean it, soldier! Like you know it. Head up. Arms stiff at the side.

SELF: All here? At ease.

Stage direction: collective breath of release, feet slide apart and form a v at the heels, hands behind back— 'we're as relaxed as we can get at this moment' pose.

SELF: HEART, please proceed.

HEART: I don't want to complain, but I thought we were a team. I've been hurting. I haven't known who to turn to. For the longest time no one listened. I felt as if someone unplugged me from a source of love. When I fell, everyone saw me on the ground and nobody reached out. Eventually, BRAIN couldn't ignore me—it was easier to deal with me than step over me every time he went out. It's ironic, though, him being the first to 'help' since brain doesn't feel. When he saw me at my lowest, he actually offered me his care, assuring me he'd take charge when the blade stabbed too deep. But BRAIN never told me how he would deal with it, or that there would be side effects. I needed help and I was willing to take any I could. BRAIN did take a weight off my shoulders because clearly I was not strong enough to deal with these issues by myself. But I now see there is a cost.

SELF: Duly noted. Thank you, HEART. BRAIN is up next.

BRAIN: Since the whole team didn't do anything when Life waved a white flag, when HEART needed us at the worst time, I had to help. I am no hero, and I didn't have any manual of how to fix things. I sat down beside HEART, and checked out his bruises. HEART made such an effort—put on a great fight. Truly, for the one that can feel the most of all of us, he's stood his ground… until he didn't… couldn't. Therefore, to help him take all that weight off, I shut off the HEART when the waking nightmares were too real. By closing the door of HEART's house, HEART didn't have to feel anything. I called it 'cruise control mode'. HEART then rendered you, SELF, a robot. Much safer than feeling and having empathy. Protect the asset. Isn't that what it's all about? And while I'm confessing… yes, it was me, BRAIN, that made BODY the mess he is. But what choice did I have? The pain had to be processed somehow. I demanded BODY laugh at horrible situations. Situations that would make a mother question what happened to her child. I rendered BODY's eyes insensitive. Any time blood flowed, any time Life left a human, I made it so BODY didn't see it for what it was. His ears stopped hearing the cries. They stopped listening to the screams for help. They were deaf to sadness. I gave BODY a rucksack to carry all the trauma in. I created a liar. "It's normal to see death, to witness abuse, to hurt," I said to BODY. Anyway, I did the best I could to handle the situation. I made it so that you, SELF, would envy those who didn't feel. When you were so weak, because HEART had broken and BODY was unable to go through a normal cycle of a day, it was me, BRAIN, who made 'us' stronger by taking away empathy and closing your eyes.

SELF: Shocking, but valuable input, certainly. Thank you, BRAIN.

Stage direction: SELF looking past BRAIN to SUBCONSCIOUS. Hey, I don't remember you in roll call. Identify yourself! Civilian or Soldier?

SUBCONSCIOUS: (Whispering) I'm just observing right now.

SELF: Speak up, I can't hear you. Name!

SUBCONSCIOUS: (Slightly louder than previous statement) I'm SUBCONSCIOUS.

SELF: (Addressing group) Yes, of course. I forgot. The quiet one. So quiet I don't always see you. Your ideas aren't always as good as mine, but let's hear what you have to say. I want to be as open as possible. And where are you based?

SUBCONSCIOUS: (Excited tone because of being asked for more than his name… expectant even.) I'm based right here, but downstairs. (Fade to whisper) You keep me out of the loop. Basement. No communication with anyone.

SELF: (Moves to the far end of the stage, engages in a monologue so the others can't hear.) He's right. It is as if I cut out his tongue a long time ago. Someone told me he had more wisdom than me. I didn't want to hear that.

SUBCONSCIOUS: (moves closer to SELF than the other characters, uses his arm to turn Jon around.) At one point in this storm, I began to scream, but no sound came out. I was mute. So I came to you in your dreams.

Stage direction: SUBCONSCIOUS turns and addresses others.

SUBCONSCIOUS: I sent cryptic messages so that HEART could unlock the code. Presented myself in terrors.

SELF: Those dreams. I wanted to run away. That was you telling me, telling us, we needed help? We ignored you.

Stage direction: SELF facing group, gesturing with an extended hand to the entire cast, drops head in shame.

SELF: We ignored SUBCONSCIOUS.

Stage direction: BODY steps forward, stands to attention, and salutes.

BODY: Permission to share, Sir!

SELF: Permission granted.

BODY: I didn't ignore. I saw SUBCONCIOUS trying to scream. I felt the effect of those dreams. I got closer to SUBCONCIOUS. He explained everything that had been muted by BRAIN.

Stage direction: BRAIN hangs head.

BODY: SUBCONSCIOUS told me it was lonely in the basement. The weight of the world crushing him. Crushing all of us. We were losing our energy to interact, to communicate, to function, to live. Not weak, but hurt. It was time for me, BODY, to do my part. But all the signals were down, so I admit it. I took it upon myself to work with BRAIN to create a way for us all to block out and pretend 'whatever was happening' wasn't happening. Like put ourselves into another frame of mind, another place and time. It was as if we created a situation of dissociation. We didn't mean to create more vulnerability. We meant to remove it.

HEART: I couldn't decode the dreams. I'd been deprogrammed so I couldn't feel empathy. Besides, I was busy snail-mailing a letter to SOUL to report the lost connection between us all—the system was down. And, I confess, I did see SOUL later, risking it all at the top of the tower. We should have all been there to hold the ladder.

Stage direction: a dark character (DISSOCIATION) at the back slinks back and shrinks even further.

BODY: It's like something invaded and took over the way we are organized. We used to be so carefree and happy. Then it seemed like a button was pressed and, after that, none of us could do our jobs. We were shut down. From a BODY perspective the shut down meant no vision, no hearing, and the tastebuds, well, you know, they became useless. Remember, buddy… you used to love eating? There was nothing quite like a great gathering with delicious food, remember? Now food just looks like an object – there is no reference to pleasure.

BODY: (moves about a bit on the stage to be inclusive to all, then continues speaking.) Honestly, I'm aware that everyone is being targeted. BRAIN doesn't work, HEART doesn't feel, SUBCONSCIOUS is mostly AWOL, and I, BODY, am a mess. It's no wonder you're a mess, *JON*.

Stage Direction: Cast remain still, but their eyes all search for JON. They look at themselves, at their own features, and look at and into each other. Which is Jon? They arrive with a fixed stare at SELF.

SELF: (collapsing a little) Please, someone drag me out of the water. I'm at the point where there is nothing I can lift to my lips to make me smile. I fear everything I once trusted. Anxiety has birthed anger because I have no control. I don't exist. I am missing in inaction.

Stage Direction: Soul floats forward. **Lighting:** Soft, pearl spotlight on SOUL.

SOUL: You all know I am here. I am the one that sometimes you don't want to believe in. Don't think I don't know that I've heard a couple of you say I'm too spiritual. What did you call it, BRAIN? A bit woo-woo? But when the spirit is broken, what is left? I have been trying to figure out a way to reach you all. When I did that, I put my sorrow on HEART and broke it a little more. BODY shed my words through salty tears from its eyes that cannot see. I have called BRAIN so many times it hurts. I've even had a tête a tête with SUBCONSCIOUS…

It seems to me that there is only one solution and that is we must work as one and, in order to understand what is going on, we must recognize the invader and understand our enemy's unit. Even work with it.

SELF: Enemy? Invader?

Stage direction: SOUL looks toward door into the shadows. Three characters emerge. The larger, one hand in his pocket, wears a wide, pride-filled smile.

PTSD: Good morning. It's always a good morning. Coffee on? I'm always ready to work. I love my job. I am Post-Traumatic Stress Disorder, aka OSI for Operational Stress Injury. My makers are still fighting on whether to call me a disorder or an injury. I've been here a while; let myself into the barracks, so to speak. While all of you were fighting to stay above water, I took control. It's what I do. Chaos is my middle name. But believe me, I am more popular thank you think. I save lives. It's complex. Yes, it's even twisted. At this point… well, some time ago… at the breaking point… you needed me. And I was assigned. Special Ops. Do not even think of calling me a mercenary. I am a serving member in good faith.

At first, I had a tent and a sleeping bag. But you didn't see my camp. You let it go so long,

I had time to get some bricks and build a more permanent structure. Between you and me, it is way harder to destroy bricks than hay… you all know the story of The Three Little Pigs. Just try to blow off everything I built up. I am more than the big, bad wolf. I am PTSD for fuck's sake. Respect me or I will take you out so fast your head will spin. Yes, that's me. Filled with cliché. Drenched in my own stink and I revel in it. Take a whiff.

Stage direction: PTSD lifts arm that is not in his pocket.

Familiar smell, huh? Thought so. I've been shitting in your bed for ages. Just wait until you see the castle I've planned—a veritable fortress. I am full of metaphor. A million therapists have tried to explain me, categorize me, define me. I morph. I'm full of surprises. I'm like a human IED. I got a PhD in fucking with your mind.

Stage direction: In fear and surprise, the group form a tight unit, in opposition to PTSD. SELF is visibly trembling.

PTSD: Now, get used to it. We're all gonna live together like a happy little family.

DEPRESSION: (as yet unintroduced) Yeh, but boss, sometimes we *are* relocated. Remember the time that doc did a number on us and we had to leave?

Stage Direction: PTSD glares at DEPRESSION

PTSD: Shut-the-fuck-up, soldier.

Stage Direction: PTSD swivels head to SELF, smiles, turns on a twisted charm.

PTSD: JON, may I call you that? Let me tell you that a great many more have died because of me than have walked away. Many an individual has tried to drown me with alcohol, but know this: I'll be back stronger the next day, and bring backup: Remorse, Shame, and Guilt. My resources are so much stronger than yours. Have you heard of a parasitic relationship? Well, I like to think ours can be parasitic-sympatico. Roommates, JON. Su casa es mi casa. C'mon, I'm bigger than a bank manager—I not only hold your mortgage, I've got your goddamned deed. (Laughing—clearly enjoying himself—in his element.) I've been around the barracks a while now. I made BODY sleep after a few hours of being up and, when night came, I guaranteed sleeplessness. I annoyed HEART so much there was a fear of going anywhere or expressing anything. And BRAIN? I messed up his office so much he can't find anything anymore, let alone concentrate for too long. Jon, you can't live with me and you can't live without me. Poor SOUL… I wouldn't call you broken… yet… but if I were a sporting man, I wouldn't pick you for my A team. Nobody likes a slow-poke or a weakling.

SELF: No. That's impossible. We are a secure unit.

HEART: Were. We were a secure unit.

BRAIN: You? You moved my files. Jammed my stapler. Found, then shredded my password list. Corrupted my hard drive? How could I not notice?

SUBCONSCIOUS: (Whispering) I told you so, BRAIN, but would you listen?

SOUL: (gently, namaste hands) Stay together, platoon, stay together. Do not blame each other.

Stage Direction: SOUL appears as if ready to lead a prayer, but PTSD waves SOUL out of the way.

PTSD: (gruffly) Do I look a little familiar? I am the bully from your childhood.

Stage Direction: SELF eyes wide. Taking a good look at PTSD.

PTSD: (stoically) I am that first friend you lost to the rope from which he hung himself.

Stage Direction: SELF shaking/trembling, eyes tearing. The platoon gathering to soothe SELF, caring gestures, an arm around the shoulder, a fresh coffee, SUBCONSCIOUS pulls up a chair and BRAIN helps SELF sit.

PTSD: (loudly) I am that moment when you fought for your life, when that guy attempted to taser you and beat you to death. Jeez I laughed.

Stage Direction: SELF recoils. Seconds later, BODY responds in the same manner. More caring gestures from the rest.

PTSD: I'll make it easy for you. I apprenticed in the battlefield. Come see my operations centre. I have a control room with multiple security cameras tracking your every move. If you resist me, I will construct a wall on your path. Let me save you the time: between you and me, you are too tired to break the wall, and you can't go around. The only option you have is hitting your head on it. This will hurt, I guarantee.

SUBCONSCIOUS: (whispers) You are despicable.

PTSD: Oh, I almost forgot. Meet my right hand man, DEPRESSION. Doesn't say much, the gloomy fellow. He's the one who insists your blinds are closed and tells you to stay in bed right when you start feeling better. He's the one with the superpower that deprives you of colour when you watch television. He is a master at creating beautiful sculptures of sadness. He is a goddamned artist and you are his canvas. When his mouth's shut, he can be a clever one, DEPRESSION can… able to remove the doorhandle on any exit. And the other one here. This is our surveyor, always sent ahead to check out the lay of the land. DISSOCIATION, give the team a wave, though I know they've already met you – they just didn't know it was you at the time.

Stage Direction: PTSD and his crew do a little back patting. SELF'S Platoon scan the surroundings, as if looking for an escape. They focus on the door. Their energy is momentarily restored.

Further Stage Direction: Then it fades as their expressions reveal there is no way out. The door is inoperable. Spotlight on a grinning PTSD (DISSOCIATION congratulating DEPRESSION to the side) as PTSD pulls his hand out of his pocket and holds up a doorhandle.

FADE OUT

CURTAIN

inhale 1 2 3 4 5 6
hold 1 2 3
exhale 1 2 3 4

from my occupational therapist
thanks, Jasmine

OPERATION: WIRED DIFFERENTLY

BRIEFING ELEVEN
OBJECTIVE: THE LAST WALL

My glass of wine tips. This is my French equivalent of the straw that breaks the camel's back.

It was autumn, 2019. A Thursday at 1645. My first shift of a four day set. I'd risen at 0300 to work out. A long day, I'd attended a few accidents, a domestic complaint that turned out to be more couple's counseling—and I am clearly not a social worker. After that, I arrested someone for an outstanding warrant; he made sure to call me all the foul names in the book.

Almost the end of my day, I headed toward the district office to finish some reports. A suicide complaint came over the radio. The CAD (computer in my patrol car) showed I was the closest to the location. I took a deep breath, keyed my mic, and told the dispatcher that I would attend. Flashing blue and red, complete with sirens, I press the gas pedal.

While paying attention to the map on my CAD, the road, the pedestrians and drivers, the dispatcher gave out information. The male was middle age, Caucasian, found by his fiancé. He had cut himself. No information if he still had the knife, if he was dead, if he was alive—and what his state of mind was. Very little information to go on other than to register there was a weapon, therefore potential danger for a first responder. For me.

I turned onto a street where a firetruck was parked outside the residence—the responders were waiting for me to make sure the scene was safe to enter.

I parked partially on the front yard. The fiancé waved to me from the front window. I ran to the house while putting on my gloves. She opened the door and pointed up the stairs. Through tears, she shared he was in the last room at the end of the hallway. Her eyes were filled with sadness and fear.

In the quick dash, I observed the house was relatively orderly and clean. Nothing out of the ordinary. First thought: a normal family.

Two bedrooms at the top of the stairs. In seconds, I registered no children's bedroom and located the scene.

He was lying in a pool of blood, still holding the knife. He was extremely pale. I immediately went to him and took the knife from his weak hand and threw it out of his reach. He'd lost so much blood.

The cuts on his wrists were the deepest I have ever seen—and I've seen enough; attended many suicides in my police time. Despite my years of training in the military, I did not check for another bleeding area. I latched onto his wrists as tight as I could to slow the bleeding. As my grip tightened, his eyes opened. I told him with my voice and my heart that I was here to help him. I was the police. That it is my job to save him. His eyes closed and he went back into the abyss. By this time, the firefighters were behind me and took over my grip. They had more tools to help him... and more training.

Seconds later, a supervisor paramedic arrived—the ones who drive the SUV and attend emergencies. She knew better than all of us, and cut away all his clothes and discovered the laceration on his inner thigh.

When I saw it, I thought: 'you are dedicated not to come back.'

Later, I'd think about how dark his world must have been when he made the choice to cut his skin.

We were six first responders in the room. I was delegated to a watcher, which meant I needed to find a job. I secured the knife. New information, perhaps from the fiancé, mentioned a firearm. I began to look for the gun but found something else in the closet. The wineglass tipped.

I knew the UN medal was associated with Bosnia. It was pinned alongside a few ribbons. He was a veteran. His clothing told a story. He was a correctional officer—a sergeant.

I could not stand the wineglass upright. I could not take the straw from the camel's back. He was my brother. A fellow soldier. He was every man I'd served with. He was me.

In less than ten minutes my life had changed. An ambulance had arrived. I heard one of the paramedics say he'd lost about three litres of blood—half of what the average body holds.

We can't lose another veteran. That's what I thought.

I called my sergeant who was overseeing the street and made him aware of the situation. I mentioned that the male was a correctional officer and a veteran; we should make sure that the victim's 'status' be recognized through the proper channel. Since there were enough hands on the male, I attended the fiancé on the first floor. I asked her about the source of his sorrow, if there was anything she could tell me. There was not much to tell. I was made aware that he had sought help with Veterans Affairs, but he didn't qualify to receive help. Clearly, someone had failed him.

I would not leave him alone.

The EMS supervisor asked me to ride to the hospital. He was still alive. There was protocol in case he became aggressive… even though he wasn't capable at this point. But, better safe than sorry.

Once again, I called my sergeant, as per regulation. I informed him that I was riding with the ambulance. I was informed that the CoC (Chain of Command) were not interested in the fact that the male used to wear a uniform, and that it was his choice to take his own life. After all, suicide is not a crime.

I informed my supervisor that I was going with the ambulance.

He told me I was not.

I told him. He is my brother. He is a soldier. He is every man who serves. He is me. I am going with the ambulance.

I don't work for the money and had no wish to be paid overtime for this. I was going on my own time. I defied the order.

I was there.
I am here now.
Everything becomes present.
That's how flashbacks work.

We are riding the ambulance and we are in traffic, trying to get around drivers who don't understand that an ambulance with sirens and lights on means 'get off the road'. I thought that the driver schools all taught the same thing: if a first responder's vehicle is heard or seen you move to the side of the road and stop your vehicle. Apparently, that is not the case. As we are driving at over 80 km/h to the hospital in the left lane, there is a driver who sees the lights and, through fear, brakes suddenly. We are lucky to drive around her. Also we are lucky not to have any recording devices in the ambulance; you would have heard me swearing in English and French.

At the hospital, there is an emergency room awaiting him, with a few doctors and nurses. I stay there. He is my brother. I want to hear that he will be fine, that he will live. But nothing.

After twenty minutes, I walk away. But a doctor calls to me: "Mister Officer." I turn. He hands me a picture from the soldier's wallet. It is of a Calgary police; an older picture, I can tell, by the state of it and the style of the mustache of the officer. This someone means something to the soldier who is in the operating room. I call my CoC and make them aware of the situation—he is our brother, and another brother is in his wallet—once again I am dismissed. I call the officers in the patrol car who also attended the scene.

This patrol car contains two of the finest police officers: kind souls, and hard workers. They work on finding the police officer in the picture. It is a tradition that, when officers are involved, fellow officers share any news. Later on, I am told that the male in the photo is the brother of the victim and has moved to another province. He has been informed of the horrible situation. I am relieved and thankful to those two finest.

Closure

One of the horrible parts of being a police officer is that you don't always know what the outcome of the situation is.

What I know is this man will live in my heart forever.

Where is my closure? I am just a high end cab driver. That night, I drove home thinking of my family. What could I have done differently or better? Why, why another veteran?

Exactly thirty days went by. Once again I was on day one of my set of four. I woke early to work out. In the past months, my workouts had been weak and unprofitable. I figured that it was just the lack of motivation. That morning, at 0834, I was downtown sitting in my patrol car and my eyes had an overflow of tears. I put on my sunglasses even though it was overcast. I didn't want the public to see something that I couldn't explain.

Clearly, something was off. I made a choice to drive back to the district office. It got harder to breathe. And harder to focus. All I could do was see the veteran who was a correctional officer. I saw his medals. All that blood he lost. I saw his uniforms. I saw myself.

I texted my sergeant telling him that I needed to meet him at his office. I called the social worker affiliated with our police service. Lucky for me, she answered. I tried to explain to her, but the words only came through my eyes. Finally, I managed to tell her that I would email her. I hit a wall and it hurt like never before.

At the district office, my sergeant was waiting for me in his office. I sat across from him at his desk, and broke down even more. I told him I couldn't do this; it was not for me. And, for the first time in my life, I had a panic attack. But why? Nothing special happened this morning. My sergeant was already speaking, saying he was going to meet me today, anyway; peers had told him they'd noticed a change in me. He gave me the option to go home and take the rest of the day to recover—offered a few hours off.

I went home. For the rest of the day, I had moments of dissociation and couldn't explain to my wife what was going on. In her eyes, I could see that she was trying to hold it together for both of us .

I took the next three days off and saw my family doctor. I have a great rapport with him. He had served in the British Army years ago and I felt like I could open up to him without the fear of being misinterpreted. Sitting in from of him, with my son on my lap and my wife by my side, I was, once again, lost for words. Only tears. My wife explained to him what had happened. I was also able to answer some of his questions.

What followed was one of the hardest things for me to hear. He said he believed, beyond my severe depression and anxiety, that I had post-traumatic stress disorder. He knew that's what would be diagnosed: PTSD.

Near the end of his own career—once a soldier forever a soldier, and a doctor—he looked into my eyes and I swear he grieved for the end of mine, ached for the journey he knew I would be going on.

There was no more joking from the crazy Frenchman who crashed the scenes and saved the people. Most of the people. Some of the people. Get off the stage. The Gig is up.

The glass had tipped. The wine was spilled.

OPERATION: WIRED DIFFERENTLY

BRIEFING TWELVE
OBJECTIVE: THE SPIRAL DOWN

Imagine this...

You hit the wall, and then you fall. To the bottom of a well. There is dank water there. No one draws water from this source. It is stagnant. How deep, you are not sure. You bring your head above the waterline; it coats your face with its stagnancy.

The sides of the well are dark, musty smelling—they could have been circled bricks laid a thousand years ago.

You must tread water. You sink. You swallow a little putrid liquid and, as you heave from its burn, while you are still under water, a human hand plunges into the cold dark and grips below your wrist. Your fingers encircle a forearm, your head is pulled above the surface. As your shoulders emerge the contrast weakens your grip. As your strength wanes, you become aware of the strain you're causing.

The rescuing hand squeezes in a way you know it doesn't want to give up, but you are too heavy. Your arm slides through your rescuer's grip. The hand snakes in tight compression around your wrist. But the darkness calls, and you slip through a valiant effort. You sink, then fight, and tread water some more.

The days are no longer days, nor are the nights for slumber. Yes, there is clock-time for appointments and schedules that you are a part of, but in some 'lion, witch, and wardrobe magic' you don't leave the well, even though you find yourself in waiting rooms.

Time has a whole new meaning… so does space… so do the senses. Pizza is chalk. Music contains missed beats. Gone is the soft scent of clean on the sheets. Your feet no longer tingle when barefoot on the lawn. The sharp outline of where things begin and end is smudged; maybe you left your sunglasses on in the house.

For me...

It began with a 'there might be something going wrong here'. Then, 'okay, I think there is something wrong'. Then, as nightmares became day-mares, continuous-mares, real-mares, there is the knowing something is wrong. But what is wrong?

The search for 'what' began. A path no one wants to take… it's like searching for an abducted child and not wanting to be the one that finds her dead, but at the same time wanting to be the one that finds her alive. It's not a search party. It's a search funeral.

There are people under the umbrella of community helpers, and there are people who work for them in supportive roles, and they are all good people with favourite ice-cream flavours, an aunt that calls at inopportune times, a preference of dogs over cats—they are receptionists, HR personnel, and even parking lot attendants—but I cannot connect with their lives, or mine. All these people lead to an office of a social worker, psychologist, psychiatrist, medical doctor.

'Can you hold please?' 'I'll be right with you.' 'Take a seat.' 'Bury your head.' 'Walk through a fucking mall so busy with people when I am at my most sensitive of sensitive to get to an office where my secrets are exposed.' 'Make an appointment before it opens, but even then, when I am finished with the appointment, the shopping centre is open.' Why do offices conducting sensitive business have to be connected to people-places?

Walking through the mall, even when it is closed, there are mall walkers, and quite a few elderly people… they might be a threat. Retirees, yes. I keep an eye on their body language, their hands… while one of mine—my hand—is concealed, holding on to my pocketknife. I might get attacked. The voice in my head is so real. It repeats that I am in danger. It looks for everything that could be a threat, when there is no threat. It is something I am trying to learn to control but when my hyperarousal comes to life, it meets up with my hypervigilance.

In that same mall, back in 2016, a man with a machete attacked people, and a police officer had to shoot him down.

I come out of the appointment and must make my way through the mall. I carry my post-therapy exhaustion and all my secrets out among shoppers; my injury a white flag above my head, a flashing neon sign above like a talk bubble that says: 'no I didn't come to shop for a pair of jeans, I was down that hallway in the professional annex—yes, where those kinds of appointments happen'. I walk—reminding myself to breathe, undoing all the good work that was just done—past the storefronts to the closest exit as if parading naked before the world, in front of all of those who are curious, career people-watchers, fearful moms—don't stare at that man, honey.

It's like that.

Breathe.

One day I fully expect that a helpful doctor's receptionist will chase me down and announce from fifty paces behind: "Wait, Mr. Archambault, you forgot this in our office." And I turn to see her holding my crumbling wellness in the form of a large-print version of the analysis of me, and a giant bottle of medication—if it did happen, hopefully it would just be my toque or gloves.

For me...

There was sick leave, then extended leave, then disability, then extended disability, then long term disability. Dis-ability. I feared I had gone past the point of being 'able'. Able to function? Able to provide for my family? Able to provide for myself? Able to love?

There are invested professionals and there are ones who have seen too many and are exhausted, and ones who have seen too few and are inexperienced. One of those is a young man and, after it is established that he and I have not 'clicked', and I have restarted with someone else who discovered that young man had clearly missed some crucial reporting, the young man is still in my periphery, because, by some evil trick of an office shuffle, he ends up in the office next to the doc with whom I have clicked. During my sessions, the young man's laughter next door is so distracting I want to knock down the wall and scream at him how offensive his laughter is, how immature his interaction is. He is probably book savvy, but clearly not street smart. Fuck, he wouldn't last anywhere outside his comfort zone.

I can't say where mine is anymore.

In my case...

Next came a mix of professionals that would eventually coordinate and share reports during the 'diagnosis' period. Part of the information they receive is from me: the patient.

But patients do not always disclose the depths they sink to in the well.

The therapists often, at first, receive an inaccurate picture. 'I have not showered in a week' may sound like I'm a horrible, dirty guy, so I don't mention that part. I am too proud. Pride is a part of me: freshly shaved, standing at attention, the uniform without a trace of lint.

My truth is becoming a façade.

The problem is, the professionals need to know those depths—they are not judging, they are evaluating. The difference between not sharing this information and disclosing all the nasty, dirty, aspects is tantamount to an incomplete diagnosis, which affects meds and therapy, which even affects remuneration—salary.

Imagine this for yourself...

There are self-ratings required on a scale of one to ten as to how you are doing. But you don't want your therapist to think you are completely out of your mind, or you are so ashamed to admit something that you fudge a five out of ten—you make a dark scenario a little brighter so you are not a complete asshole.

Apparently this 'fudging' is common in the self-rating system. But, their need to evaluate is dependent on your disclosures. Their advice, be it medication or other treatments, includes taking this score into consideration. But since you were not 'honest' the prescribed solutions are based on misinformation that you provided.

But that's not all: even if you were honest and five out of ten was a clear rating you'd given yourself, next week's score you give yourself is not comparable to last week's because the scale is always a moving target. This shit is too complex to assign a number to it.

The tests do not reflect the reality of the sickness. They do not allow for the range of scenarios. Home is a comfort zone: few triggers, if any, unless you count the fear of going out. Reality is when you leave home. The threats are out there. Everywhere out there. The person driving behind you is following you. Bonjour triggers. Paranoia is now your drink, your water.

Imagine this, too...

There are a stack of forms to fill out. Some folks will slip through the cracks because they are in their home, their fortress, not able to come out of their room to open their mail, not without the support of loved ones. Sure, they may have insurance, and be grateful for it, but if form A is not filled out before 'date A', then you might be shit out of luck. What if you were in bed that week? What if you never fill out a form at all? What if you can't?

How will it be possible for you to fill out forms that include a home address when you have forgotten what home means? 123 Darkness Street, Bottom-of-the-Well?

You will use one hand to hold the pen and the other to tread water, so where will the form go? If you hold the paper and the pen, then you're going under. Newsflash: ink and water do not mix; they cannot make clear words. You can't make spaces between the words. Those spaces are your breaths.

For me...

The papers float away. The pen sinks. I tread water. Another hand reaches my wrist and pulls me up, but I manage to catch the pen and wet paper and push it to them and they take it somewhere to dry out and fill it in for me. When they return, they do not always have the strength to pull me out; when they do, I don't have it in me to hold on.

Then there are the moments when the hand is small and golden. My heart breaks when it shines through the dark; I have to close my eyes or I will surely die from love. It is the hand of my son. I will not pull him under. I will tread water and be strong next time when the hand is that of a therapist.

But when it is the hand of a therapist, when my shoulders have emerged, and the connection is strong, a clock appears and our time is up for the session.

I keep treading water. I'm so tired of the water. Maybe that's why I stopped showering.

"Crazy French policeman on the scene." I will diffuse this situation. I'll stop this assault. I'll rescue myself through humour… wait, I cannot. I am no longer a police officer. I'm no longer a soldier. Where is my uniform? With no uniform, who am I? Hey, up there, those whose hands reach into the cold black and clasp mine, who do you think I am? What am I to each of you?

Tread water. Stop. Swallow. Gulp. Resurface. Choke. Flail. Tread. Who am I to me?

I have hit the bottom, sort of, but I can't go up. Someone remembers there is a ladder attached to the side of a well. Their message and direction arrives in coaxing echoes. It is an old ladder, they tell me, but if I can get to the side, find it in the darkness, there is hope. A torch is shone to the choppy waves I've created from treading. It is blinding. But

I spy the ladder. I make my way and cling to the wooden side rail. A swarm of tiny slivers sting my hand. A chunk of rotted wood comes off on the other. No matter. I cling. Find my footing. Secure myself on a rung. I must be gentle with this relic.

One. Step. Just one, Jon. My clothes weigh a ton. I'm so cold. One step exposes my shoulders. I wrap myself close to the wood and cling to it, resting my chin on a rung that I hope to reach in a few more strokes. And I weep. All I have known for the past few years is treading water. Treading water to the point where it felt normal. I should never have gotten to that point.

One. More. Step. I feel the crunch with the sole of my shoe—I know what sound it would have made if it was not underwater. The rung has split. I'm back where I was before, on the first step I'd found. Clinging to the ladder, a larger step to get to the next rung, which may crack too. And what about the one I'm on? How long before I'm treading water again?

There are slivers in both hands. I'm terrified the ladder is going to come away from the wall.

I have to live with this. I may die with this. I don't want to die from it.

Chronologically

Before we were married, before we moved west, my time off was shared with my soon-to-be-wife and friends. There would be a storm in the kitchen as I cooked for everyone. Wine flowed freely. Bread was broken, not sliced, and consumed in yeasty mouthfuls between laughter and chatter. Sauces were simmered then slurped. Military brothers and sisters and their partners grinned, satisfied. They would grab my head in their hands, breathe garlic into my face, and kiss my cheeks, one, two, three times, and say bonne nuit, Archy.

In my life, food was une fête—a celebration. Then, one day, flavour was gone. I grieved its loss: the process of dough rising; the burst of a new world beyond the door of a boulangerie—the closer to the ovens the thicker the aroma of baking baguettes. I mourned the absence of the pleasure of butter, cheese, a chocolate milkshake, a juicy hamburger.

In November 2019 I stopped exercising. Endorphins that had been regularly generated, even during my decline, were no longer an option to access. I could not pull myself together for a walk.

I'm not sure when I closed the curtains and blinds in the house. Perhaps I had been closing them for some time, and my wife opening them behind me without realizing I'd been trying to keep them closed. But on November 29, 2019, I wanted all the light shut out. I had to have it that way.

I don't know when I began to dissociate either, but I have a clear memory of one day, when my wife was working away from home, and I was at home with my son, that I snapped out of another world and heard his voice calling to me. The safety gate across the bottom of the stairs had toppled on him, and he needed me. I hadn't seen or heard him. It scared me to my core.

On a cold November 2019 morning, my sergeant had sent me home for the rest of the day, his message rebounding in my head: you used to be so happy and chippy and now your teammates say you're jaded and negative. I'm glad you came in. I was going to ask you to come in anyway.

The rest of the day? How could I get myself together by tomorrow?

The rest of the day? Something was wrong. Maybe the blood tests I had done in September showed some kind of illness, and they'd missed it.

The acronym PTSD was not in my mind at that point. I took three sick days during which I arranged to see my doctor.

Counsellors, psychologists, therapists, and social workers cannot grant time off for a person even when they believe the person requires it. Only medical doctors can do this. When I called for the appointment, I was told my doctor was away. The administrator made an appointment for me to meet with the fill-in doc on December 3rd.

My wife accompanied me to the appointment, our son in tow. Children have a way of brightening a room; they create a buffer. By default, their presence reminds their carers of parental responsibility and, in turn, strengthens that parent.

The doctor's youthfulness surprised me and, in hindsight, I wonder if I was instantly concerned about burdening her. The assessment began with a single question that even a toddler could answer: "How are you?" Those three words completely overwhelmed me—I would not be able to get through it. I attempted to share my fear of being judged that I was weak, that people might think I'm making this up—whatever 'this' was. Then I began bawling: a dad in a complete mess.

It's okay, son, daddy is a little bit sad. It's okay for little boys and big boys to cry.

My son accepted me for who I was. So did the doctor. My wife caught all the words between my tears and strung them together in coherent sentences in a compassionate translation. She was strong for me. She was strong for our family.

On December 3, 2019 the fill-in doctor advised that I should be taking two weeks off. The letter to my sergeant cost $75.00 because there is a fee when you are sick. Yes, a fee when you are sick.

The next two weeks were spent in a state of exhaustion and confusion. I didn't know what it was like to be 'home'. I had not felt 'home' since I left my parents' house at seventeen. My overtime hours alone for that year were in the hundreds. Even when my son was born and I took some paternity leave, I worked part time for the military, then returned to the police service earlier than I had planned.

Looking back, I recall my wife saying to me that I seemed to be happy then, working part time in the military, back with my 'family'. She said I should re-sign. I don't think she was joking.

When my family doctor returned, at the end of my two weeks off, he took control. A clever man. A caring man. I was so comfortable with him. He said, 'I know you. I know this is more than depression.' He went on to explain, when all this was examined, that he knew the diagnosis would be PTSD.

It's not what I wanted to hear. I wanted to hear that the results of a blood test showed that I had 'xyz disease', easily cured by a course of antibiotics. I'm sure he wished he could have said that too. Fortunately, he is a brilliant man and I trusted him; at least there was some comfort in that.

A former military man, he insisted I go to Veterans Affairs as they were a better one-stop-shop, took care of their own, and were familiar with PTSD. He made it official with a letter that I would be off for six weeks, taking me to the end of January 2020. He did not charge for this letter; he said, "we are brothers in arms."

I didn't tell my parents at that time. I just wanted to keep this to our own small family. Fuck, the truth is, I didn't want to tell myself.

There were times when drinking was more than a friendly pint or two with a buddy. For some, a bottle of golden elixir becomes the 'drink me' in an Alice In Wonderland moment of disappearing, of becoming so small that not much can fit into the remembering part of the brain.

There were scheduled days off, before I hit the wall, when there was only time to sleep to catch up and go back on shift again. Sometimes 'that' sleep was aided by alcohol. Though it was a short period of time, there is no doubt I used to it self-medicate. Most soldiers know the powerful effects of the kind of twisted therapy a drink or seven can provide. What sustains can also kill.

I began to think about what the end of January might look like… me going back, in six weeks.

My employer received notice that I would be on leave, and be involved in therapy related to PTSD.

The saying goes that the pen is mightier than the sword. The few characters in a text message I received on December 15, 2019, after being off for sixteen days, was like a switchblade catching me off guard.

"Hey Jon, just so you know, I will be going into your locker to retrieve your service firearm and mags. As you have been off for more than 30 days and not expected back before 60 days has elapsed. As your tentative return to work is Jan 29. But of course that depends on your doctor and whatever time you require. Your pistol will be stored at firearms and available when you come back."

When I caught my breath…

I was so raw. Completely fragile. A psychological blow: that gun was not a weapon as most know it, but a tool of my trade. Part of my uniform. Already vulnerable, I was now being disrobed—naked among my peers. Weak for all the world to see.

Interestingly, when I was on paternity leave—scheduled for three months—nobody took my firearm.

Eventually, I was asked for the uniform. A trusted member who lives in the same town as me returned it on my behalf. I couldn't go in. But eventually, I had to go and clean out my locker to make room for someone else… even though I might be back, some day, even though I received calls from another department—a perky person within HR, asking when I was returning.

In those first weeks, I reached out to the Operational Stress Injury Clinic for Veterans Affairs. OSI indicated they'd set me up before Christmas 2019, but I did not get a call from them to meet that schedule.

I was determined to make sure all the t's were crossed and i's were dotted, even though I didn't have the energy or focus to cross and dot. When we moved west, to serve the community, we had taken a significant income cut. My wife started over.

The sacrifice of the move was financially challenging. The next blow—being off with the operational stress injury—delivered a forty percent cut to my current salary.

Receiving sixty-percent of my salary created another level of stress beyond financial. It created an administrative labyrinth through which to navigate. I'd never had to think about how that might work. I'd never seen myself 'on disability'. A subset of services within the Workers Compensation Board, and the insurance company affiliated with the Calgary Police Service each required different forms, multiple appointments, and a coordination of all the red tape. Easier said than done.

Christmas 2019 was not the season for me to be jolly or bright. There was no New Year's party. Nor were there shifts when I would usually be on the job, dealing with the darker side of the holidays. At home, I ***was*** the darker side of the holidays.

Highway 2020 – The Road To My Hell

Medications were started the day I saw my family doctor in December. I had never been on medication before. Some of those I've since been on are:

- *Venlafaxine*
- *Bupropion*
- *Sertraline*
- *Escitalopram*
- *Prazosin*
- *Quetiapine*
- *Seroquel* XR

Throughout January 2020, as I waited for OSI to contact me, I was in touch with the social worker I knew from the Calgary Police Service, and I joined a group of first responders with operational stress injuries. We met in a large house associated with a non-profit organization that is dedicated to first responders and military. It was a relief to be in a neutral group and hear their stories. While I felt reasonably safe within it, I was exhausted from attending so many appointments which included seeing my family doctor on a regular basis.

Around that same time, I discovered that the young social worker I'd bared my heart and soul to had not passed half the information I'd shared, and he'd reported I was not suffering from trauma originating from my military career.

No trauma?

I don't think I'd finished shaking my head over the 'no trauma' thing, when I learned that my medical doctor was retiring. I didn't want him to. He knew me. He referred me to another doctor who used to be in the military.

Though I connected with the new doctor on some level, he had only served in the military because, while at medical school, a recruiter presented him an option to have his education costs covered.

He agreed I had a problem—*no shit Sherlock, I know I have a problem. As if I don't know something is going on inside of me.* He had a plan he said would 'fix' me. I was eager to hear.

He'd barely opened my file when he delivered his solution: back to work… right away, as in immediately. That's what he believed I needed… back in the trenches, boy… stiff upper lip… that which doesn't kill you will cure you.

It is one thing to go back with the boys in the field while serving in the Forces, it's another to return to policing the streets of Calgary.

Despite my explaining it was not safe for me to be on the job, and that it was not safe for society, he was on the 'back to work train'. *Light 'em up. Sirens full blast. Go get the bad guys. A soldier's work is never done.*

His ears were closed. His eyes were shut. *What if I get into a fight? and I try to control and apprehend someone? and I lose it? What if I give someone too many punches because I am angry… because I am raging? What if I do something I would regret? Wait, would I regret giving one too many punches to a criminal?*

When I caught my breath, I decided to find another doctor. This is not an easy task in that there is always that respect thing in the back of one's mind that says: 'all doctors are right', 'doctors are superior', 'doctors know better than their patients'. And many doctors have full caseloads.

Two Steps Forward

Within the week, I discovered, through a neighbour, there was a new doctor in town. He was taking new patients. I met him. He was willing to work with me. We clicked. I wanted to trust him from the get-go. I could tell he trusted me. He had the power to say whether I could return to work. I was supposed to return soon. My six weeks was coming to an end. He was clear in his directive. Another month off, and meds. I was to keep seeing the social worker.

In a glimmer of administrative, professional, and heartfelt humanitarian intervention, the social worker with the police, formerly an OSI employee, stepped in and made a recommendation. She shared there was no doubt that I had PTSD.

The wheels began to turn.

Note: The psychologist I saw was through the 'neutral group sessions' which were attended in a large house—not in an official office. I was seeing the social worker from CPS once a week, and trying to get required appointments with the OSI clinic, but there was a wait time.

Though I didn't have a lot of energy to go to all the appointments, I was scared that I would be told I was faking my stress if I didn't take advantage of all that was offered to me. I made sure to have as many appointments as possible. Maybe it would heal me faster? I know it sounds ridiculous, but that is how it was for me. It wasn't sustainable, but it is what I did… out of fear.

As mentioned at the beginning of this book: not every psychologist can work with every patient or client, nor can every patient or client work with every psychologist. The relationship has to work and, in the name of health and wellness, for the benefit of both parties, it is imperative that the connection work. In my own situation, over time, I have been matched with some professionals with whom I had that disconnected feeling. This didn't make them bad people. I met with an ex-football player who had worked in the prison system—a terrific guy. But I was self-empowered to ask for someone else to make sure the fit was right for me. This was respected, even encouraged by the professionals. It does no good to prolong the process or compromise your healing. At a time in your life when it is hard even to get up, let alone advocate for yourself—hopefully someone supportive is on your home team—it is crucial to be able to speak up.

In February 2020, I readied myself for an appointment with the OSI clinic—a psychologist was set for another intensive intake. It was cancelled because of Covid. I continued to attend the group meetings of first responders who are dealing with their work injuries, and see my new family doctor bi-weekly.

In the meantime, and on into the future, including at the time of writing (2021), medication trials were and are ongoing. It takes time for a medication to leave the system, time for another to show if it is working. Trials of meds, and the transition time between, is a road through hell. Wait, scratch hell; the disorienting journey, at times, makes hell look like paradise.

In January 2020, my employer moved me to long term disability.

Disability.

Words Matter

Sickness versus Injury. Wellness versus Illness. I had never been one to be too concerned about political correctness—respect yes, but trending terms, no. Yet I could see the effect of labels and the language used to describe mental health and vulnerability.

It was early days. I was still operating under a paradigm of 'you are weak if you talk about your feelings'. But I was beginning to understand that this was not true; it's just lots of people believe it. I began to discover how much strength it takes to live with the effects of trauma. I was grateful, daily, for my wife's fortitude and dedication, but I'm not sure that my gratitude showed. I was difficult to deal with. I pulled away. She pulled away. We were both terrified. Our son brought his happy self to every day, yet the responsibility of parenting, and on the days I couldn't parent, the weight of understanding I wasn't parenting well was crushing me.

Jon, We Have To Open The Curtains

By March 2020, the world was understanding there would be major changes to, well, everything.

Though it was not clear to what degree this would affect lives and livelihoods, the cracks in our systems began to be exposed. Global vulnerability, and division that goes along with that, began to become evident for every single individual on the planet.

One small rectangle of fabric with elastic loops each side rocked the world as it became the catalyst, excuse, and scapegoat for human beings to choose a side, to politicize something much larger, to publicize extremes of opinion. Every day, a full moon.

Every moment the zombie apocalypse was about to knock on the door of our world.

In a way, the impending restrictions were music to my ears. I don't have to go out. My inner-demons celebrated. *We've got you now, Jon.*

My wife announced there would be light; said it was time to open the curtains and blinds. If I wasn't going out, then the outside needed to come in.

Mission-oriented, I did what was asked of me. With the windows revealed, the house opened its eyes to a winter landscape, but that was an invitation to be observed and exposed—I didn't want to look out, and I didn't want people to see in. I retreated to my office. Installed a lock on its door. I may have been defeated, reduced to one room, but this was my military bunker. My own. And I knew I was making myself a safe space.

But even a soldier has to come out of the bunker from time-to-time. On less stressful days, within a low range of the scale of tolerating the rest of the world, I established a pattern of booking appointments. To avoid people, I'd schedule things at the beginning of the day or, in the case of a haircut, right before closing time. The fewer people around the better. I drew on my military trade, becoming a master logistician and communicator for the 'conditions' I was operating within.

About the barber shop: there was I time when I took my son to the barber and three police officers were getting their hair cut. My heart started to race, my vision narrowed, and I had to walk out of the shop while the clerk was talking to me. It was rude to walk away, but I needed to. I couldn't even trust my own brothers. I was under attack. No one could see it. I looked like a dad with his young son, but inside me I could barely function.

EARLY PANDEMIC 2020

It is May 2020. We have been in a form of lockdown, confined for the past eight weeks or so. I have observed the news, read about this pandemic and how people are reacting to it. I see in society the sense of emergency: gathering more toilet paper, food, and other products that they feel they must have. I have been to the grocery store and seen people fighting for bread and cleaning products. Instead of sharing and getting together, the pandemic has brought out the worst in some.

Certainly, getting out of my 'fort'—my house—triggered me. Seeing people fighting activated my rage and aggression. They were fighting for useless things, creating a war for toilet paper. Am I the only one who knows various things can be used to wipe one's own ass. The civilians were not following any rules of respect. When I'd paid for my goods and driven home, I sat in my vehicle in silence for a few minutes. I didn't want to enter my house with the weight of anger on my shoulders. And… I was sure I had forgotten something and I didn't want to disappoint my wife once more—my memory (damn the meds and PTSD) is not as effective as it used to be.

In my vehicle, I had time to reflect on my previous therapy session with my psychologist. Just to be clear, all my therapy sessions are on Zoom®, which is fantastic for my safety. He started the session by asking me how I was doing in this confinement—pandemic lockdown. I recall smiling at his question. I replied that I was totally fine. Perhaps deliriously so. I wanted to stay at home because inside my fort I am not triggered as much. My omnipresent hyper-vigilance is not as active in my 'fort'. Ironically, I could see my neighbors becoming more stressed at not being able to go out, not being able to have people over.

I was totally fine with confinement. I didn't have to explain to anyone why I won't be attending any dinner, any event, any 'thing'.

What came to my mind was: everyone out there can finally understand a bit more of my world.

Right now, I had time to focus on my family, myself, and maybe try to figure things out. Still, I couldn't escape everything. Sometimes, being with myself too much revived old methods of coping. I had the desire to drink until I blacked out, or I had the urge to sit on my balcony and frantically smoke a whole pack of cigarettes.

Fortunately, I have since been able to reject those demons and focus on writing about them. Who knows how long the pandemic will last?

Jon, if it weren't for our son,
do you think you might have taken your life?

I still will not answer that question.

ANOTHER DAY, ANOTHER DAY

I woke up this morning. In my mind it was one more day when I have to get up. I hear my son crying, screaming 'Daddy'. My vision is blurry, not only because I just woke up, but because I took a hand-full of medication to tame my anxiety, to kill my night terrors, and supress some of my post-traumatic stress. I take my phone to text my wife who is in the basement, working out. I text her: "I'm up." That way she knows that I will care for our son. Like most of the population, I hope, I brush my teeth.

I don't feel happiness or sadness, it is a numbness. I remember a time when I felt joy, but it is a long time ago. Oh yeah, I have to get my son from his room. I am a robot. I am on cruise control. I remove his sleep sack like most mornings, change his diaper, and put him into fresh clothes. Then I bring him downstairs.

I prep breakfast for him and for me. Nothing too crazy. Meanwhile, I listen to music—I will steal the feelings from each song.

Lately, there are only dark songs. Those are the only ones my soul will let me choose. The music is more than a distraction. It holds me in its arms. It transports me.

Music—a single song—feels for me. A playlist can provide real respite. This is because I don't know how to feel, what I feel, or what is going on inside me… because I can't express myself about what I feel, because I don't know how to feel.

Though I don't know how to feel, I am still keenly aware I should be. It's like there's a knife in me and, if I remove that knife the blood will gush, but the knife has to be removed in order to begin healing—I know that much. But I cannot pull out the knife. Not right now. It's holding me together.

What I can do is immerse myself in the lyrics, throw myself into the singer's pain. Only then can I breathe. Breathe with the beat. Even if it is only for three minutes.

Playlist: let me escape in your art. Bring me into your fold. Cover me with the blanket of your poetry—a patchwork quilt of your own heartbreaking stories. Let me wander in your gallery of darkness. Dark and heavy.

Heavy hurts.

My son is in his chair, his belt is secured, he has food and his Tablet. I am fully aware that I should not keep him too long on the Tablet. But I only have so much energy.

He is eating. I put some mindless show on my cellphone: auditions from Britain's Got Talent. Boom! I am gone. (Don't ask me what they were singing or what they said.) I have taken a trip to the Land of Dissociation. While I was there, my wife came upstairs and talked to me. I heard nothing, even though she was less than a metre away.

When I return from the Land of D, I don't blame her for being upset. But, I feel no guilt. I guess the medication supresses that too.

One second I am there, and the next one I have teleported to la-la land. I can't even imagine how my wife hates this rollercoaster, or hates me.

Link to my playlist, The War Within, created for this book: https://open.spotify.com/playlist/7Jmt6iMidC7pkjB077B2nT?si=TieuG036QkuMgG5dVXeK0w

One Step Forward, Three Steps Back, Change The Meds... And Again... Rinse And Repeat... How Long Is This Road?

Every New Year is supposed to bring change. People commit to the gym. Quit smoking. Lose weight. And even though they might not stick to it, they have the power to change. That choice to 'be well' or 'not to be' is a choice. There are two options.

But for those with PTSD and OSI every day is a first and last. Every night is preceded with a different countdown.

For me, along with side effects from the meds: not being able to have a proper bowel movement, zero sex drive, no taste when I do eat, and elevated blood pressure. I either sleep too much or sleep too little. Dozens of other symptoms come and go. I am the poster child for PTSD, a mad scientist's chemistry lab within my body, mind, and now—I fear—in my soul.

During 2020, I reconnected with military friends, and lamented the loss of others. The topic of operational stress injuries, PTSD, dissociation, and mental health issues became more relevant. Not only was I living it, but no first day of January, or any other special day, was going to offer itself to me as a day to choose change.

PTSD doesn't show up and ask to come inside. It lurks outside, surveys its surroundings, and then breaks the door down. Despite being on seemingly never ending trials of what meds would work best for my symptoms, I fought hard to maintain some semblance of a productive day-to-day. I worked on balancing on an ever shifting deck of a boat on choppy water.

And as I entered various stages of grief, mourning the inevitable loss of my career—few people asked when I was going back to work. People didn't always know what to ask me or say to me. Hell, I didn't even want to ask myself the question, since I was pretty certain of the answer. But, some days, I entertained a few creative ideas. They were all in the realm of service to others. If I couldn't wear the uniform, I could still serve it. I could help, as Jon.

Parallel with that creativity, were other imaginings that I told myself were practical, necessary, yet heart wrenching scenarios. How could I expose my wife to this every day for the rest of our marriage. Those vows traditionally include 'until death do us part'. I was dying , (or was I already dead?) in front of her most days. She deserved 'a life of freedom' not a 'life sentence'.

In my creative space, I began to write poetry. Dark. Real. My experience. Then, I began to attach to the idea of sharing an important message to Canadians, Americans… anyone who did not understand the cycle thousands of first responders have had to deal with, survived, died from.

These ideas would develop into a number of initiatives.

During that time, sometimes, in the hours I could project a future, I danced with the idea of a book.

In May 2020, my psychologist said that I would not be going back to work. "You don't fight a ten year trauma injury in weeks." The professionals involved made the official diagnosis of PTSD. While that would be honed with other specifics, it was a turning point of sorts. I needed to hear it, even though I didn't want to.

As I fought to accept my wife had a disabled husband, I sensed she was being careful around me, and I wondered if it was to protect herself. I wanted her to be safe. I wanted to be better. For her. For our son. For me.

During the summer, still at the bottom of the well, still unable to climb out, I continued to get used to different meds for sleep, anxiety, and myriad other symptoms. I began to manage my situation (within the well), as energy permitted, and a new, but difficult, life began to emerge.

It didn't show up every day. But there was a seed of hope that I could manage the PTSD and still have times of productivity.

I was still at the bottom of the well, but I was used to clinging to the falling-apart-ladder. I even think I might have become more buoyant. Though I would look up past the bricked walls I could not climb out.

During the summer and fall of 2020, as my son sprouted and began to be more boy than baby, I worried for his future. And for my wife's. I was not being fair to them.

The depression ebbed and flowed, but never ceased moving about me in relentless waves. Sleep was near to impossible. I became accustomed to a strange existence in which hope and my family was all that got me through, but the waking nightmare was that I was putting them through hell; their getting me through was exhausting for them. How the fuck did people deal with this when they didn't have anyone in their life? When they'd never had someone know them before their injury? My heart broke for all those individuals. But then, I imagined myself as one, sort of: living apart so that my wife and son could move on with their lives, but I would still have a family to live for.

I worked hard to be a family member. Though I still wanted to be in the house, I wasn't always in the office. The door was opened. I walked with my dogs, but constantly looked over my shoulder. And I wrote. And I established an online presence. Sure, I was exhausted and had to take naps, but there was some purpose to this injury that had paralyzed me.

Still, within the Covid environment, I was able to participate in various therapies. I also realized that what I had done, for a long time, was work to make everyone happy and then put myself last. I had adopted the priority of Special Forces, and set my life's priorities they had told me to establish: the missions, the unit, the members. I began to wonder if all the overtime I'd put in as a police officer might have been done to ignore that something was wrong.

As my wife and I moved into the new reality, I was overwhelmed with pride and admiration by her growth, her spiritual journey, her unfathomable strength.

I began to feel I was in the presence of a magnificent mountain, complete with streams, pines, deer, bear—strength, balance, courage. In awe, and filled with gratitude I could not and still cannot always express, or thankfulness that gets diluted by medication, I kept considering an ultimate sacrifice of sorts. To offer her a way out: open the door for her to the freedom. I began to think on it.

I wrote more poetry.

I began to recognize I could be supportive to others while I managed my own issues.

I started to feel more comfortable leaning on my brothers and sisters.

I pushed myself when I could.

The work on the book took shape.

RAGE (outbursts of aggressivity)

My view is that the military is too proud to explain rage. It may be that they simply don't have the words. None of the books I've read share a visceral process of rage—not from a military-mind perspective. Sure, there are works of fiction that are psychological thrillers crafted with unhinged characters, vindictive actors, and crazed serial killers, but what about real life, and the rage that kicks in, from seemingly nowhere, in the life of a person like me?

I enjoy driving my blue Nissan Murano. It's an extension of me, the driver's seat molded to my body. We operate as one: the angle of my leg and foot on the accelerator, the span of my arms from shoulder to steering wheel seemingly customized, as if we were designed for each other. When I look out of the clean windshield, check the mirrors, and pull into traffic, we are a proficient unit.

So relaxed am I, having just attended therapy (mental health) and wrapped up a trauma, that here in this vehicle it's almost like being in my home on a good day. For the first time in ages, contentment and tranquility is present; it's as if Serenity is sitting in the passenger seat. It's a privilege to be driving such a revered guest.

It's a wonderful thing, Serenity and me taking in the sights. Outside, nature displays incredible gifts—there is still some gold clinging to the branches stretched out in late autumn, and the mountains on the horizon are topped with fresh snow, their sparkling peaks meeting a clear, blue sky.

I am in a movie where the hero's journey is complete. He's battled the demons, saved the world, at peace with himself. There's even energy to use the hands-free and check on a friend's wellbeing. Serenity smiles an approval—seriously, she's birdsong herself—then she points to a majestic red tailed hawk on a fencepost.

Serenity, I love you—we should go on a road trip.

My friend picks up on the third ring.

"Hello," he says. There's the kind of relief in his voice that comes from receiving a call from someone who cares. Serenity gives me a thumbs-up and mouths, 'you're a good friend, Jon'.

The road to the Foothills town I call home is a narrow-shouldered, two-laned, two-way. It's not much further to my house. Instinctively, my foot eases off the gas pedal; ahead, the grey Subaru Forester moves about 10k under the speed limit—Ontario plates. They must be unfamiliar with the road. "'Whatever," says serenity. "The ride is still enjoyable, no? We have more time together."

She's right, I'm in no hurry. I want to stretch out this inner-peace as long as I can. Serenity throws back her head and laughs in the kind of way that warms my heart, the kind of tone that says life is good.

Over the phone, my friend chats casually while I compartmentalize our conversation, separating it from my driving.

I smile and check the rear-view. There's a twenty-something in a silver Mercedes sedan closing in. The boy's impulsivity, impatience, entitlement, and greed rides my bumper. Ahead, Ontario is leisurely touring—oblivious to the necessary safety around consistent traffic—but it shouldn't be a problem because they're up front and can set the speed at whatever they wish based on the conditions for them. Mercedes Boy pushes. Now I can't see his headlights. My colon twists—he's in my ass.

Every hair on my neck discovers a life of its own, prickling instantaneous hate. Fuck you, kid. Vachier, va te faire foutre.

I turn to Serenity to ask her if there's anything she can do about this. Could she flow her form into the Mercedes and slow him the fuck down, but she is gone. Maybe she anticipated my request and has got this.

No such magic. I can only see the boy in the Benz.

The line to my buddy remains open. If he is speaking, I cannot hear him. Nor am I talking to him.

Ontario maintains a lazy slow, blissfully unaware of the danger behind. Mercedes slides to the centreline ready to blow past. There is no passing here. It is not safe. You fucking moron, there could be innocent people coming the other way. Get back behind me and slow the fuck down. Serenity, where are you?

He pulls out. He's not allowed to do this. There are only two lanes—one in each direction. Mercedes Boy is almost beside me. You effing asshole. You spoiled brat. You immature son of a bitch. Ah, tabarnak d'osti.

"Jon, what's happening? This sounds serious. Please, you're gonna hurt someone or yourself." (Through the speakers.)

Frame by frame in slow motion—the result of adrenalin flooding the system, so every movement, feeling, and all surroundings are thoroughly noticed—the stage is set. Tarantino couldn't have directed a more intense scene.

I accelerate and block Mercedes Boy from passing, swerving in front of him. I leave the tourists from Ontario in the dust. There's plenty of room behind my Nissan for the kid to avoid a head-on. Hey! There are only two lanes you fucking asshole. He remains on the wrong side of the road and, rather than tucking in behind, comes up beside me, determined to pass. The oncoming driver is aligned for a collision not of their making.

No fucking way. Calis d'ostie de tabarnak.

"Buddy, what's happening?" (Through the speakers.)

The approaching vehicle is straight and steady, rightfully in its own lane, and closing in. I will not slow. Get behind me you fucking cunt.

"Jon, listen to me. Whatever you're doing is not worth it." (Through the speakers.)

I have no hands. Well, I do. I can see them gripping the steering wheel, but all feeling—fingers, palms, wrists—is gone.

I am acutely aware of the scenery around the car, both lanes, the ditches. Ontario has U-turned. The silver steel of the luxury car is right beside me. Die, Mercedes Boy. The world is better without you. Fuck you.

He accelerates, I keep up. We're doing 160. So clear is the yellow line that it looks as if it has just been painted.

The approaching car is upon us. There is no time to let Mercedes Boy ahead of me, even if I wanted to, which I don't. There's no time for him to go behind me. He swerves onto the opposite shoulder and partly into the ditch. I watch it all, only the oncoming car between us for a nanosecond as it stays in its lane.

Roll. Die you bastard. Lay bleeding in your Mercedes. I'll not be coming back for you. You son of a bitch. Fils de pute.

"Buddy, Jon, are you there?" (Through the speakers.)

The sounds of rage are no longer audible curses but guttural grunts. Where are you, Serenity? If only you could have stayed. Help me.

Mercedes Boy bursts out of the shoulder and ditch and blows ahead of me.

I. Am. So. Not Done. With. You. You fucking bastard. I might as well be in police pursuit, but I am no longer a policeman. He tears around a traffic circle, I mirror him. I'll rip you apart you son of a bitch.

I tail him at high speed to a residential neighbourhood where he quickly turns onto a driveway and, out of fear, panic, or both, must have previously punched his automatic garage door opener so as to escape. *You idiot. I now know where you live.*

"Jon, are you there? Jon? Jon, buddy, you still there?" (Through the speakers.)

Idling in front of Mercedes Boy's home, I re-engage with my friend; tell him the enemy is hiding in a garage. My friend tells me he's been shouting to me the whole time. He says, while he can relate, for fuck's sake, it's over. **"Go home, Jon."**

I drive home like the dedicated, safe dad and husband that I thought I was, that I want to be, that I sometimes am not. I park in my own driveway. Minutes later, in the house, I'm drinking a glass of water, continuing my day as if nothing has happened.

More dangerous is that I have no capacity to process the event—don't even know I should be. Regret is not even in my vocabulary.

*****

The next day, at an appointment with the psychologist, I retell the incident in a relaxed manner, adding a bit of lighthearted humour. The doctor asks me if I am clear about what could have happened. I say that I'm completely aware: I could have beaten Mercedes Boy senseless.

"No," she says. "I mean what could have happened to you, Jon?"

"I don't care," I say.

Four days later, I am with the psychiatrist. The psychologist has told him the story—thanks, Team Heal Jon. It remains that I feel nothing—in my mind, during the event, the boy deserved to die.

The psychiatrist echoed the psychologist's concerns: the twenty minute road incident remained unprocessed.

My body, mind, and perhaps even my soul, had engaged with such fury—and gathered so quickly into a storm—that rage flooded every cell. It was the equivalent to the stories about a mother's instant and monumental strength, lifting a car to release her trapped child. In my case, it wasn't strength for good, it was strength for destruction.

Even scarier was that I hadn't dissected any of it, so there was risk in the future—who might it be next?

These kinds of changes bring on consequences; the psychiatrist says: time for new meds. The new pills numb me. For two months I have no feelings. Over Christmas, I watched my son opening gifts. I smiled—but felt nothing. My heart and soul had checked out. Fuck these meds. Fuck the previous meds. Fuck. Fuck. Fuck.

*****

On reflection, it wasn't like 'rage' was personified as Serenity had been, rage surged within me. I could not converse with it. I didn't become rage, rage became me. Red flags. Danger. Caution. Man without control.

My goal is to be healthy. I disclosed the incident initially, even though I was making light of it, for a reason. I needed to understand myself and my actions. The doc changed my medication… to help… the team sees me as a threat. In the future, every time I meet with one of them, the first thing they ask is, 'are you going to hurt someone?' How long will they be asking that stupid, fucking question? Do they believe I would tell the truth if I was a threat? Do they think I'm such an idiot that I'd incriminate myself? A threat to whom? Society? Myself?

The meds further suppress my feelings. Even possible excitement is MIA. When I see someone for whom I hold respect, enjoy friendship, and dearly love, I know I should feel more, but the meds rob my biology of emotion for safety's sake. Am I even human anymore?

I have a friend who once said she heard this in therapy: "One time I was trained to protect you, now I am medicated to protect others."

Is this how it will always be? Where is my lively spirit? My lust for life? Please, science, for fuck's sake don't take away the poet inside me. It slowed the writing of the book. My editor would send me things to review and I would not even open the mail. I would not care because how could I write a book about feelings when I feel nothing.

I long to chauffer Serenity again but, having said that, she is an intensity I might not be able to afford, given that her contrast, Rage, may be on call at the other emotional extreme. Give up one, give up both.

My wife and my son are the most important people in my life. For now, perhaps for always, rather than hope for a passenger, I will look at my speedometer, to my hero, my reason for living, my motivation to heal—a small photo of my son smiling at me on the console. Visual therapy.

This Makes Hell Look Like Paradise

At the end of June 2020, the psychiatrist from OSI adjusted my diagnosis. PTSD with dissociation and major depressive disorder. My medications were reviewed.

In July 2020, I met, face-to-face, with the psychologist and he introduced me to ART (Accelerated Resolution Therapy). It wasn't a fit, so we tried EMDR (Eye Movement Desensitization and Reprocessing). I worked at home on understanding trauma. An occupational therapist became involved. It was almost too much. So many appointments. Exhausting.

Another New Year, 2021, and I was still 'that guy with PTSD', 'without a uniform', and I was still at the bottom of the well. Yet, I was believing that I was on my way out. I knew that PTSD, the well, this life, would be a part of my forever. The new me. Not exactly the makeover I was looking for.

The book neared its final draft. Though it could not offer a shining light at the top of that ladder, it did begin to show a lantern inside the well. I made connections to other creative projects, using the tentacles of the artist which has always lived inside me.

We Talk

It is hard to figure out how long I have been sick. It is now 2021 and I would guess that my first trauma was in 2009. It didn't hit home at first because I felt so special to be part of such a team. Doing something I was not allowed to speak about… every boy would love to be James Bond… maybe I was… for a few hours.

My wife. My wife fell in love with me, with a go-getter, someone who doesn't look behind, someone who goes through walls and deeply takes care of others. Now it is clear that the man she met was never the whole me; a man who didn't know he was sick back then. The man who wrote her poetry is real, and when he did that he was also well into the trauma game.

How can I explain to her that, 'yes, it is me, but also it isn't?' How do I explain that I am way more sensitive than I thought I was?

In the past four years, I have moved her across the country, and so much has been asked of her while I rode the work train.

I am not the warrior. She is.

She has been fighting with resentment, hate, and misunderstanding of how and who the fuck her husband truly is.

I have hurt her, not physically. My anger is so volatile that it scars who she is. I am not angry at her. I revere her. She is my lighthouse. I am mostly angry at myself, for not understanding sooner what was happening. But she receives the wrath.

I am breaking her.

She never signed up for this. She signed up for love. How fucked up is that?

Now that we know there is a term for what is going on with me, it still doesn't change a thing. She now understands why I am this way. But she still has to live with it.

If I am sick of it, so is she. Strong as she is, having a partner who lives in such despair affects her.

I still wonder why… why is she still here? She could have left months ago, years ago, taking our son because they simply needed to step away. I would have not stopped her, because deep inside of me… I know I am a monster… I know she is not happy… she is here because she loves me.

But what kind of price is this love?

We have talked about divorce…

I don't want to hurt her.

I don't want to be the reason she cries.

As much as I love her… I want the best for her and if it is to leave me… I would support her doing it.

She didn't ask for such hell.

She is not the one injured is she? I am injuring her by being with her.

She always gets the shit end of the stick. That is because my house is my safe place. When I go out, I have on my façade. She doesn't get to see me that way: the façade Jon that can appear so nice.

We talk… we decide she should be able to see that part of me, even though it is the façade, it is the 'nice Jon'.

At home she receives the Jon she never wanted in her life. The world sees the good Jon, because they see the Jon with the façade. In our home, she can only see the real me—which is me being safe, being triggered, being raw, being jumpy when she rounds the corner of the hallway.

She deserves to see me outside.

We talk… we decide that since I am not afraid of bears, or trees falling on the car, or anything in nature, that I can show her who I am when we are outside of the house and in nature. It is the only place I will be able to show her, because I am afraid of people.

We talk… we decide we will go out to the mountains, grab a bagel on the way, then take ourselves out of the car, crunch the snow on the trail beneath our boots, weave ourselves between the trees, swing our arms around the trunks, smile, throw our arms around each other and kiss while our son looks up where the treetops meet the sky and calls out, "Look, Mommy. Look, Daddy. There is a bird up there." And then we can take him up in our arms and we can squeeze him between us and all look up to the sky together.

We need these moments.

Those with Operational Stress Injuries have become so used to taking care of others, that when they arrive home they have no energy for themselves or their family. The whole unit crumbles.

I became so uncaring to myself, that my body finally said, "Fuck you, Jon. If you're not going to recharge your batteries we'll make you sicker and sicker."

I hate myself for who I am. I cared so much for others as a first responder, that now I don't even know who I am as a father. I can't remember how to hug my family, and my wife is terrified how I might respond if she hugs me.

We have talked… we decided that we will go out into nature. Our couple's therapy, family therapy: nature is going to provide that.

We have talked… we may engage in official couple's therapy as well.

LET ME PLAY THERAPIST

Joe Canada. This is how incredibly destructive it can be. It is harmful to wait too long to seek help. I don't care about destroying my life, but I care about destroying my wife's and son's lives. My son sees me angry, and it will eventually create anxiety, due to him never knowing how his father will react. I hate myself for it and, right now, I am aware of it. The bomb is ticking… I am ticking… when is the next time I will explode? Outside my family, when I get angry, I don't care if I hurt people. The reason I don't hurt them is because of my family.

Recently, a friend told me that I seem to be so much better. So much more relaxed and grounded. I am such a good actor… I can mask so well that I don't even feel sadness. I am a liar; fake because I am so ashamed to not be me, to not know who I am now. I told this friend that, a few minutes before seeing him, I was crying my eyes out, just because someone had asked me via text, 'how are you?' and that I had to answer, fine. FINE is not a state… is not a feeling…

Every week, I sit in therapy. I am asked if I want to hurt myself and I say, "No… my son is my rock, my wife is my lighthouse." Have I thought of it? Yes… hell, yes. Because I live in hell right now… it couldn't get worse. I say no because I know what would happen if I said yes. I am aware of the road it would take because, as a copper, I took people to the hospital who had suicidal thoughts. I know the process and how it works. I would be brought to the hospital, searched (in case of weapons), locked in a room, and maybe have to stay at the hospital for days… or weeks.

Let me play policeman:

A peace/police officer can apprehend and convey you to a facility without a doctor's or judge's order (under a Form 10) if they have grounds to believe you are not complying with a Community Treatment Order, and you:

- have a mental disorder;
- need to be examined for your own safety or others' safety; and
- it would be dangerous to wait to receive a judge's warrant.

Look at that… I'm good for 2 out of 3.

For that reason, I keep it quiet. As I said, I am a liar. I wonder if sometimes it would be easier to close my eyes. I am my own worst enemy.

First responders, like those in the military, are muscle cars. We are hungry for speed; an adrenaline dump. A muscle car is made to go fast. Cruising slowly only reminds the driver that the engine is screaming for more. But, like a muscle car, always going at 200 km/h will blow up the engine, or, at that speed, if the road takes a turn, there will be an accident—crash and burn.

Right now, I am still looking for the parts of me on the side of the road, but I forget what I am supposed to look like, so I can't even reassemble myself.

My wife shouldn't have to visit that accident scene.

Nor pick up pieces and try to put them in the right place.

She doesn't know who I am anymore. Me neither.

Enough Of Meds For Me

I could go on about the side effects of medication, about the numbness, or becoming oversensitive on other meds. The rollercoaster of being sick, the rollercoaster those meds are bringing me on because, when you stop one, you have side effects. When you start another one your body has to readapt to the change and loss of chemicals.

In January 2021, I went to bed one night, and just didn't take my meds. The next day I woke up and decided to stop the anti-psych meds as well. I could hear my psychiatrist giving me shit. But I had had enough of all of it. I don't know if I stopped them because I was giving up, or if truly I was hoping for a better result. Something had to change.

The first few days were okay… I mean they were fantastic. I felt happiness. Yes, happiness. It came in the form of a smile to my lips. I was looking at my son who was building something and he was so proud and happy and… I… smiled…

For a few minutes, I wondered if it was my mask that I was wearing… then a warm wave lapped against my heart… and I knew… the happiness was real. No mask, just pure joy. Well, guess what? I cried.

The following day, I was able to work out for a full hour. Now it sounds silly but it was a huge win. Day three, I dreamed. No nightmares. No waking in sweats, no shaking, no hyper-stress. I spent a good twenty minutes reviewing my dream to make sure I was not just ignoring the darkness of it, but there it was: no darkness in that dream. That same day, I worked out again. Yes, I said it: AGAIN.

Day four… I was dizzy beyond belief. Like when you are drunk, but without the fun aspect of being drunk. I had to lie down nine hours during the day, without sleeping, without noise, without anything. It was too much. Day four ushered in withdrawal. Sadness knocked on my door… I cried… and cried. For what reason though? Only God knows.

My psychiatrist was not angry; totally fine with it. She respected the fact that I wanted to be happy… to dream, to be able to be me.

In the brightness of the new 'no medication' my anger had not left, and the conversation of divorce came to the table. I felt like I was getting off a rollercoaster only to climb onto another one. It was not my wife's fault; it was entirely mine.

Onward

When I hit the wall, and began therapy, I asked my psychologist: "Can you just tell me how to turn off this way of thinking?"

Hundreds of hours later, I'd still like to know. It would be the holy grail of therapeutic breakthroughs.

March 2021 saw me meeting with a new psychiatrist. My calendar is still filled with appointments with various professionals—and that's okay.

There are days when I can truly see progress—that work on the ladder, one rung at a time, is bringing me closer to the light. I have been building my strength and energy to confront and attack—full on—the sickness. I have no way of knowing if that will take months or a few years, but I guarantee that I wont give up.

Progress For The Current Injured And Future Understanders

I won't give up on me and, if you are also suffering, I won't give up on you. If you are like the owner of the feed store, the guy mentioned in an earlier chapter, I won't give up on you either. Your compassion and willingness to learn will help us heal.

I am asking you to be honest and, the next time it is asked, remove your mask, and speak. You don't have to scream, write a book, or create a brand… but you owe yourself that: the spoken words. It is okay to not be okay.

If the storms come to you, and the sea feels deserted, scream. Brothers and sisters, I swear to God one of us will come to help. We are family. It takes someone really strong to say, "I am not okay."

To the ones who wanted to learn about the darkness of those tunnels… of being down in a well… of the nightmare: I hope I was able to paint a good picture for you. Writing over 200 pages made me visit so many feelings; it was, in a way, therapy. And it allowed me to advocate… and hope…

… I hope you may have changed your mind if you believe mental illness was or is something a person can be snapped out of, or think that a handful of medications can fix a mind fractured by trauma. I hope I dispelled some of the negative representations of mental illness.

THE SOLDIER STILL IN ME

Maybe I have always been a soldier.

There was this time, when I was in Montréal after returning from Iraq, that a mature woman—in her late sixties—came face to face with me outside a butcher's shop. The air was crisp enough to suspend the scent of all the lamb, pork, and beef that escaped each time the door was opened.

Her expression was a combination of wonder and relief; she clearly recognized me.

"Jon? Jon? Oh, Jon, you're back," she said. "From overseas. The war."

In an instant, I knew I did not know her, but she was so certain she knew me that she made me want to believe it. "So good to see you, Jon. You're back."

"I do not think I am who you think I am." I stumbled with my words. So powerful was the look in her eyes, and strong her emotion, that I could almost feel I was 'her' Jon from another war.

I wonder if there has always been a soldier in me. I know there always will be. And I know that there is a husband, and a dad, and an artist, and a writer, and an advocate.

We are all evolving toward helping each other—lifting and carrying people so they don't have to die because of a broken femur—tending to each other so no one is left behind. The mark of civilization is caring for each other. In that way we are all soldiers and civilians.

From one civilized human to another, I am deeply thankful for you to have read me.

Link to my playlist, The War Within, created for this book:

https://open.spotify.com/playlist/7Jmt6iMidC7pkjB077B2nT?si=TieuG036QkuMgG5dVXeK0w

I ignored the past…
But like the race between the hare and the tortoise
it caught up to me
but contrary to the ending of that story
I won't let my past win…
I have faith… in me

THE LETTERS

Dear Society

I have something to ask you. Could you spare a little time for me? For so many others? Could you put some time aside for thought, please?

Sadly, the movie world—in order to shock, and line its pockets with gold—often portrays the victims of post-traumatic stress disorder and operational stress injuries as if they are humans wearing ticking bombs. The media has taught a massive following to fear those of us who have PTSD. I will not deny that we have received training to go to war, to handle weapons and combat situations. I mentioned before, some of us will face anger; there will be a few who create a dangerous situation for themselves (and sometimes for others).

It is one thing that the government, organizations, and industries are giving money for mental health; it is another thing to have the support of society. It is important to have that support because we who are diagnosed with PTSD and OSI are your neighbors, brothers, sisters, cousins, friends, and colleagues. We are close to you, and we might have kept quiet because we feel we have to when, truly, the only thing we need is ears to listen to our story.

Accept that we are also part of your society. You don't have to, and can't, change us. We are fine with learning to live with ourselves. I am not asking you to save us, but to support us in this darkness. I am asking you to live with us, too.

I have faith in you, Society, because I have seen the world change and, even in the horror of war and criminals, I have seen good.

Remember, you might encounter a first responder or military person who is not as patient as you think that person should be. You may be involved with a police officer who will not accept your excuses. Perhaps you will be in the company of a firefighter who is angry at you for doing something that could endanger your life. It might be a military member who just can't take a conversation. If or when you do, please remember, it is not about you. Truly it is not. It might be because they have attended a call before interacting with you and they haven't had time to digest the event, to process the trauma, because this kind of vocation doesn't allow its people—those who serve—the transitional time to come to terms with it all.

We never know what is going on in the life of others.

Lastly,

If you have a friend who has been 'off' lately, and you can feel in your gut that their behaviour or responses are unusual, pick up your phone, dial their number, and check on that friend. It may be the difference between their decision to harm themselves, or to give up, or to be in a darker place for longer. It might save their life when they hear your voice and know that they are not alone.

To The Leadership

Many of us joined the first responder and military world to make this rock a better place for our loved ones to live on.

The world of the first responder, including the military, has been present for years. The need to help others and respond to those who help others is a part of our heritage. More than that, it is within our human makeup. In other words, it is what makes us human.

Proof of that is offered by the great anthropologist, Margaret Mead. When asked what she thought was the first sign of a civilized culture, she said that first sign was found in a femur (a thighbone) from the remains of a human in an ancient culture. The bone showed evidence of healing from a break. She went on to share that, in the animal kingdom, if you break your leg, you die. You cannot run from danger, you cannot get to a water source to drink, you cannot hunt for food, and you become easy prey for other creatures. What animal can survive the period a broken leg takes to heal? The healed femur tells a story: someone took time to stay with the fallen, perhaps bound the wound and splinted it, fed the person, kept them safe through their recovery. Civilization starts when we help each other through difficulties. Civilized, caring people serve.

However, the helping and first responding became an industry. Carrying our fellow brothers and sisters, supporting communities by tending those who have fallen, has become big business. And in big business, people become numbers. Those who are cared for. And those who do the caring.

When 'their' own members become physically or mentally injured, those very individuals who serve to help others in their time of need, first responders are seen as a burden by the industry. Their seat is not filled. Someone has to pick up the slack. Some members begin to experience frustration with the perceived 'weaker' in the ranks. Others are terrified to say they are breaking because they will be perceived as weak, then they will be hated. They will even hate themselves. They will suffer silently, or they will speak out and suffer a different way—reminded they are a number.

The industry becomes like an insurance company and the first responder who is fallen becomes a liability. The relationship changes. The fallen responder now costs money and affects the bottom line. But the fallen responder has filled a position that is critical to the culture, essential to the citizens. A role that has its members who become numbers confronting danger—mentally and physically draining—daily, nightly, weekends, holidays.

We have to put a bit more human in this coffee…

Those who stopped to carry the individual with the broken femur have carried so many, wrapped so many wounds, fought off so many wild animals, that they have now fallen. In their hierarchy of ranks, and in their communities, they are left behind when a simple acknowledgement of 'let me sit with you and help you figure this out' would be enough to start healing their fractures.

Of course, I understand that an injured 'employee' costs money. I get that some injuries are recurring—can scar someone for life. But is money something we should put ahead of the human in the uniform?

Many at the top of the chain of command are disconnected from the reality of fieldwork. They are eager to take the glory. They do not want negative media—and what is more negative than an injured responder who is walking evidence that the system has faults.

Post-traumatic stress disorder does not sell. It's not sexy to put that on a poster.

Heroes look great on billboards. Many of them can not speak because they are now buried. They can be revered for having served because they are now quiet.

I am so proud of all my brothers and sisters, living and passed, who served and gave and served some more. There are a whole bunch of injured who do not fit the image of the ideal first responder, the saver of lives, the strong, brave, and diplomatic soldier. They make the 'company' look bad. Their voices make people 'feel uncomfortable'.

Many in their ivory towers forget that real people, not numbers, have put stone upon stone to get them there.

Leadership, you have the power to change the present and usher in a new future. You, Leadership, should be taking care of us. Bind our wounds, carry us to the stream to drink clear water. It is your civilized duty.

The leader that I learned the most from told me one day:

"I work for you. I am not there to make myself shine. If I take care of you (the team), you will make me shine."

Mental illness can't be fought alone.

Demons can't be fought alone.

Criminals can't be fought alone.

We are a team, from the bottom to the top, and back.

Evolve your leadership… Change the posters… and teach the future leaders to promote transparency, to recognize the signs that someone is near the edge, to physically do something about it, and to be fluent in compassion toward fallen members.

Like every Leader, I recognize you make mistakes, you are human and have faults like all of us. You have a heart, you have a calling, help us. Rebrand the company.

Memo To Operational Stress Injury

Operational Stress Injury, let me address you directly: go fuck yourself.

I have spoken about you in well over forty thousand words. I hate all the memories you took away from me. I despise that, because of you, I can't remember the day my son took his first step. This book is not to throw you flowers, it's to educate others about you. I want people to understand that you are not a friend, and that you are not someone who should hold anyone down.

People who are suffering need to understand that you are not in control of their lives. Yes, you slow me down. Yes, you made me re-route my life to something that I had never expected. But thank you, because, in the process of hurting me, you made me stronger. You made me realize that I owe myself more credit.

I went through a storm and blizzard. You brought darkness to a life that was aiming for the sky. I fell down with you as a partner and I am getting up with an army of soldiers who, like me, decided to fight against you. You were the spy who got into my life, spying on my weakness, on my pride. I thought you were a malediction, a bad spell. I thought you a witch who had thrown a curse at my life. Truly, I am the one who gave you that power.

I am responsible for this life, for what the future will bring to me, for all the walls I will have to break. Because I take responsibility. If you try to come back stronger in the future, I will be more prepared, and I will bring war with me. I might fall again, but I know now that I can get up and confront you.

Our relationship is over.

Dear Spouses, Children, Family, and Friends of Soldiers

Spouses, children, and close family and friends of soldiers, you are the heroes. You fight in solitude. You often are missing the fourth wheel of your vehicle, and you understand the term sacrifice because, while you are missing that wheel, society—including those in other countries—gets more from that missing wheel than you do.

Some of you will face long stretches of time without that precious person by your side. Some will feel the strain of shiftwork as several nights in a row your loved one is on the job. Many of you know the anxiety of a sleepless night due to the concern over your partner being in potentially dangerous situations.

Words cannot express the respect I have for all of you. The world often forgets about you… I have not. You are in my mind because I have seen the sacrifice you all make behind the scenes, all the times you place patience in front of frustration, respect for your loved one's career over your own loneliness and isolation. You are in my mind because I see and hear you.

Dear Natasha:

Years ago, you said 'yes' for the rest of our lives. You married a man wearing the uniform. You were proud, and I believe you still are. I made you move four thousand kilometers from your family, away from your comfort zone. You had to adapt to a new culture, to re-create yourself, and find a new job. A month after you moved here, we were pregnant with a little angel. Fast enough, I became sick; I was not really able to communicate what my heart was going through. You faced an enraged man. I was angry at life.

Nothing would stop my wondering why I had to go through that, after giving so much.

Many times you had no words to comfort me, but your presence was a balm, an elixir, life-support itself. You did not leave me alone—which I'm sure would have been the easier way. I remember saying to you that if you had to leave I would totally understand. Despite how sick I became, and how much I changed, you stayed.

You are the hero here.

You always have been.

In a gentle and patient silence, you hold our family.

Your creativity astounds me.

The world is at the doorstep; you are a brilliant entrepreneur.

And you manage the business of me as well.

And build our son—infant to boy—with a foundation of compassion.

I love you beyond the realm of any love I had once dreamed of.

And I hate that my brain and my heart don't always speak to each other when I want to express that love.

You never complain.

You supported my deployment and prepared our wedding by yourself.

You work on understanding me even when I don't understand myself.

You suited up, fighting by my side.

And became scarred in the process.

You refused to leave—said we are in this together, Jon.

And I am sorry for bringing you into hell.

Je t'aime.

Although we are living under the same roof, you have had to be a single mother because I was and am not always present. I have thanked you many times, but it can never be enough—that kind of gratitude cannot be measured. Even this letter to you, a symbol of my profound reverence, can never come close to expressing my true appreciation for who you are and what you do.

You are still here. I could thank God, but truly you are the only one I can thank here. How did you do it? How do you do it? I truly don't know. I only know you did. And you do.

Merci, thank you… you have my heart and love. I wouldn't want to do my life without you.

Sweet Lochlan

You are currently three years old—I imagine in this moment you are playing with friends at the daycare. Innocently drifting through playtime, yet there is something you do not know—though I often wonder if you feel it.

You are the one who holds my life in your hands.

You know, your grandfather went through something when I was a child; I remember part of it. It was a tough time and he made it through, for us. I am going to make sure to educate others, and you my angel, about self care. You will not have to battle these same demons. You will be able to recognize the signs of stress in yourself, therefore in others; I don't wish for anyone else to experience this.

I am hoping that you don't remember any of my struggle. I hope you will always see me as invincible, determined, present, and responsive to all.

I always wanted to be seen by you as courageous. A man that you could look up to and tell your school friends that your dad is helping others.

Lochlan, in my darker days, when I was ready to give up on life, I saw your blue eyes, I heard your laughter, and it made my heart beat with renewal. It hurt, but in a good way. It reminded me that I was still alive, that I was not totally dead inside.

When I had those moment of anger, I looked at your picture on my cellphone through my tears and I had a smile because I had you. I wanted to see you grow up, get to those teenage years when you will defy me, when you will think you are stronger and more knowledgeable than your father. I want to see you reach great heights when challenges are put in your path.

I will always be proud of you.
I will always be your father.
I am your father and guide.
Whenever you will need me,
I won't be far.
Always by your side,
Never in front or behind you,
Because without knowing,
You saved me.
You are my little hero.

RECONNAISSANCE

Natasha

Thank you for being there every day
from sunrise to sundown.
You are a wonderful mother and wife.
You are forever my most beautiful adventure.

Paula C

With deep appreciation.
You showed me how to be a leader,
even if sometimes my mouth would bark loudly.

Chris C

Thanks for telling me that
I needed to get some help
when nobody else could or would.

Andrea

Gratitude
You pushed me to put my ideas on paper.
You believed in me.
Then you knew who I should meet.

Marie

Gracias
You read all the words.
Pulled more from my heart.
Then curated all the exhibits.

Richard

The pen may be mightier than the sword;
the administrator behind the
scenes knows how to use both.

Papa

Merci, merci d'avoir été si dure et
de m'avoir poussé à aller si loin dans la
vie. Tu es l'exemple d'un homme qui a réussi,
qui a changé le monde. Tu m'as enseigné
comment être un père et un homme. J'essaie
de faire la même chose pour mon fils. S'il
te plaît, embrasses maman, elle est
aussi exceptionnelle.

ABOUT THE AUTHOR

Jon A. Archambault is an emerging advocate for those with OSI. His passion for art and history is evident in how he has chosen to deal with his own diagnosis. He and his wife and son share their home in Alberta, Canada with a small pack of large dogs. This is his first book.

Made in the USA
Middletown, DE
28 April 2021